# PICTURE BOOK OF
# ANIMALS

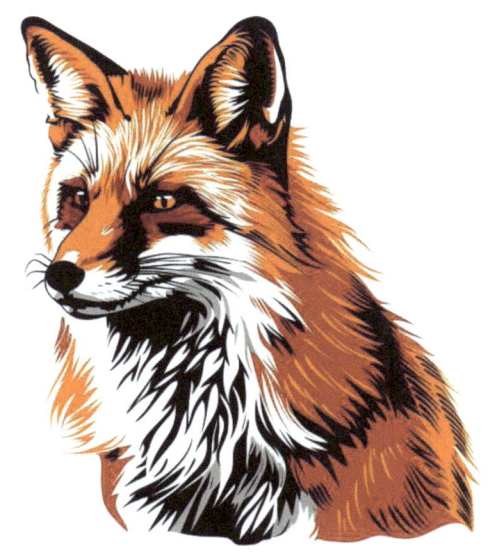

...By...

Ella Caldwell

Copyright © 2024. All rights reserved.

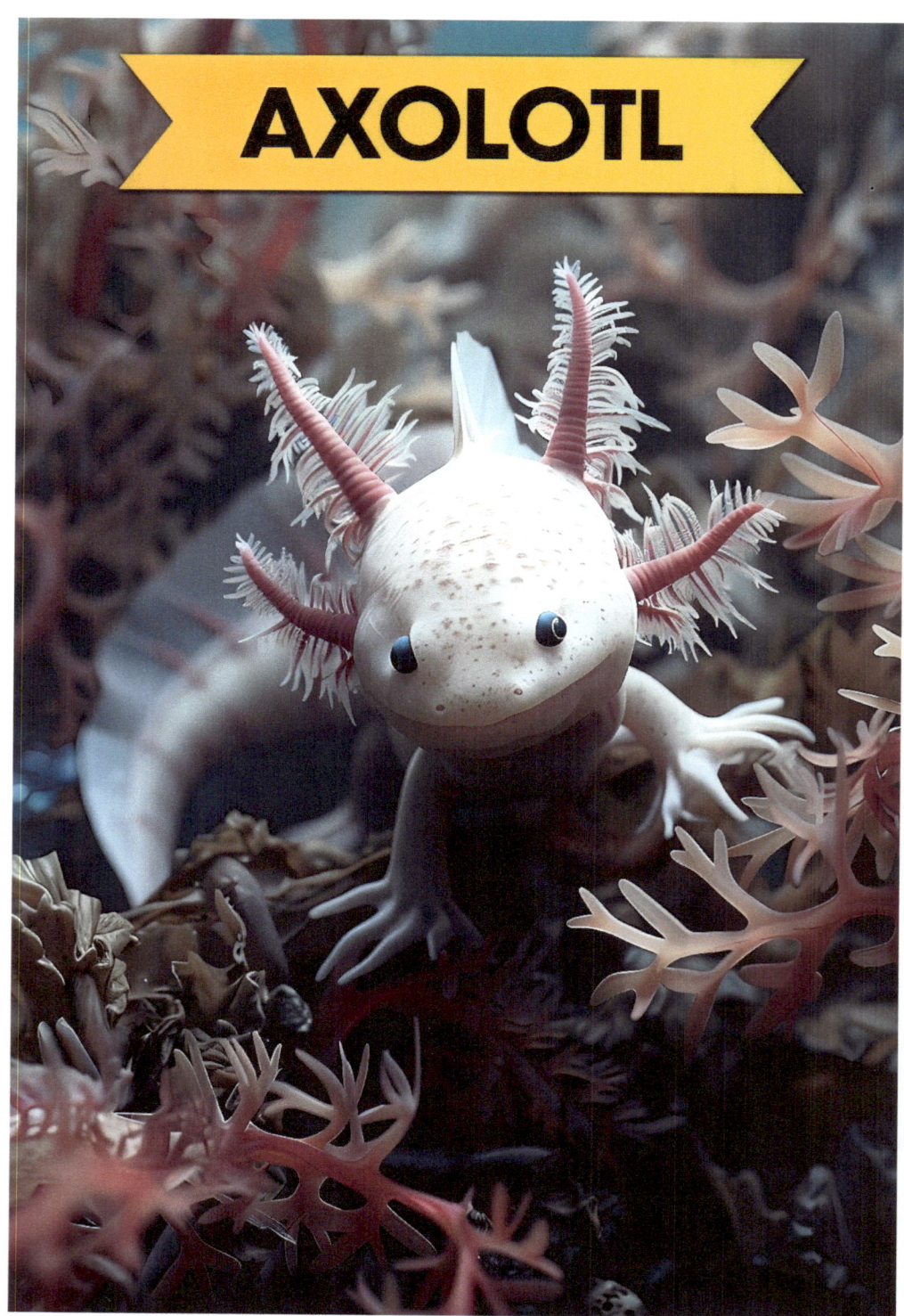

# AXOLOTL

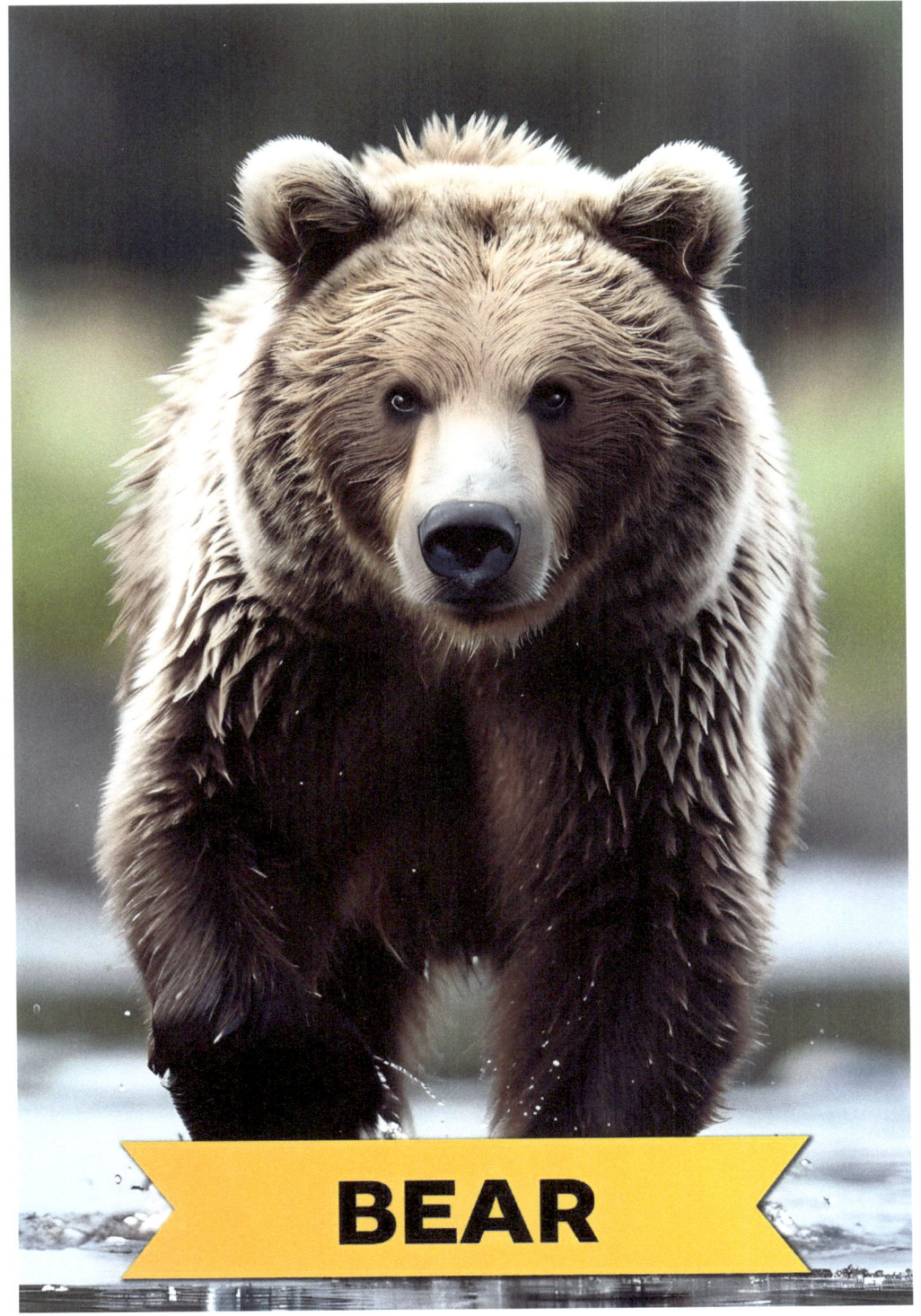

**BEAR**

# BEAVER

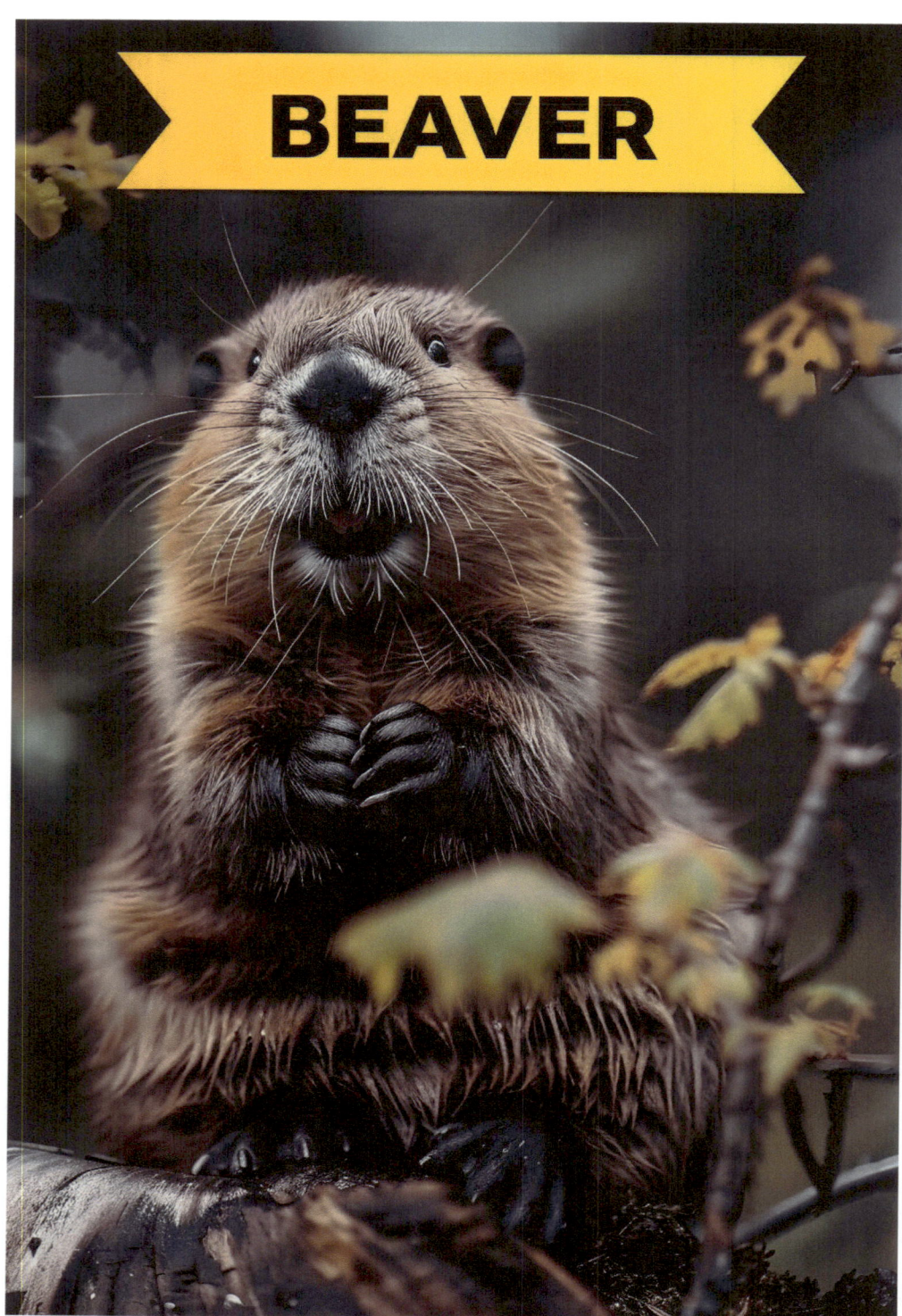

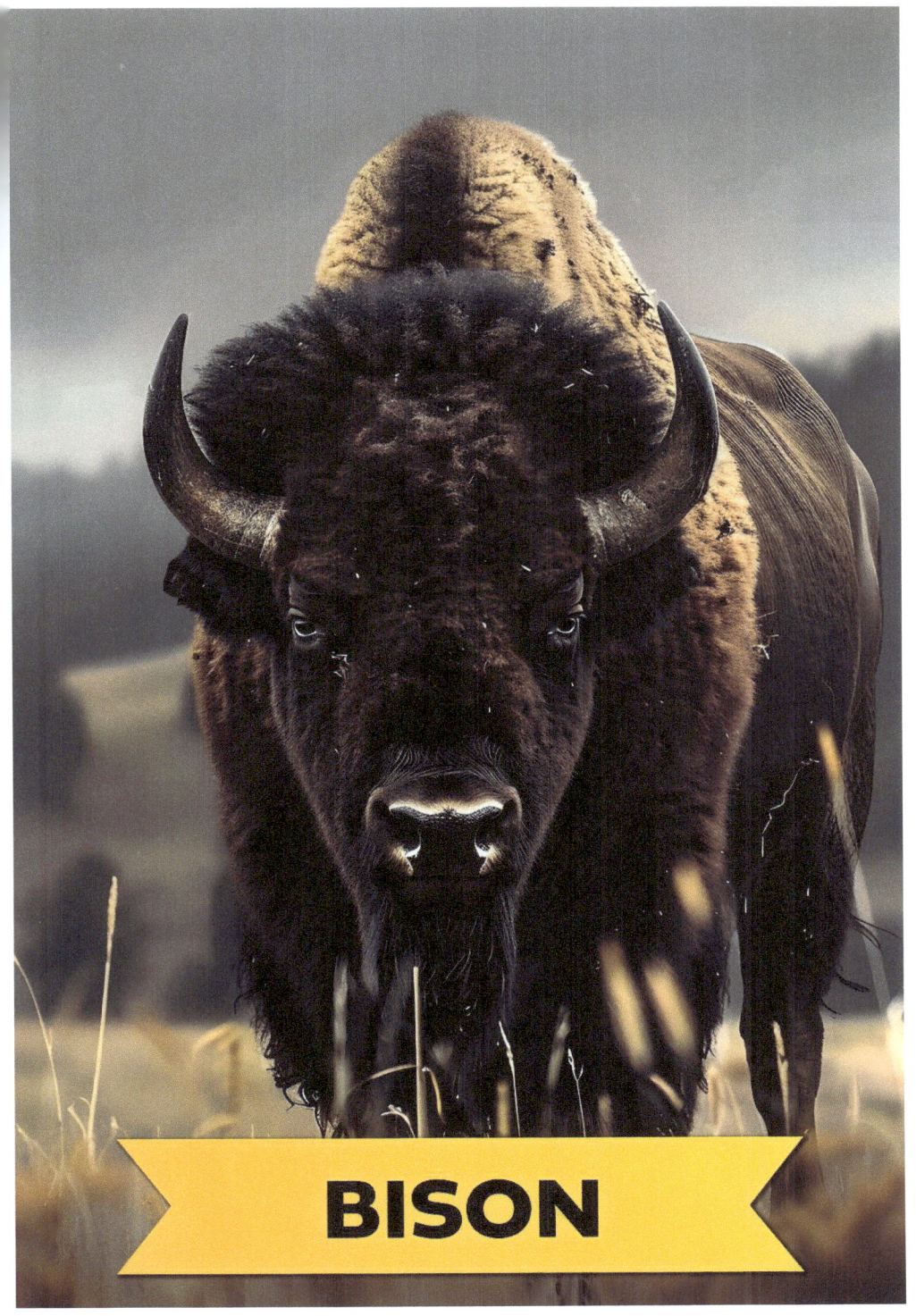

**BISON**

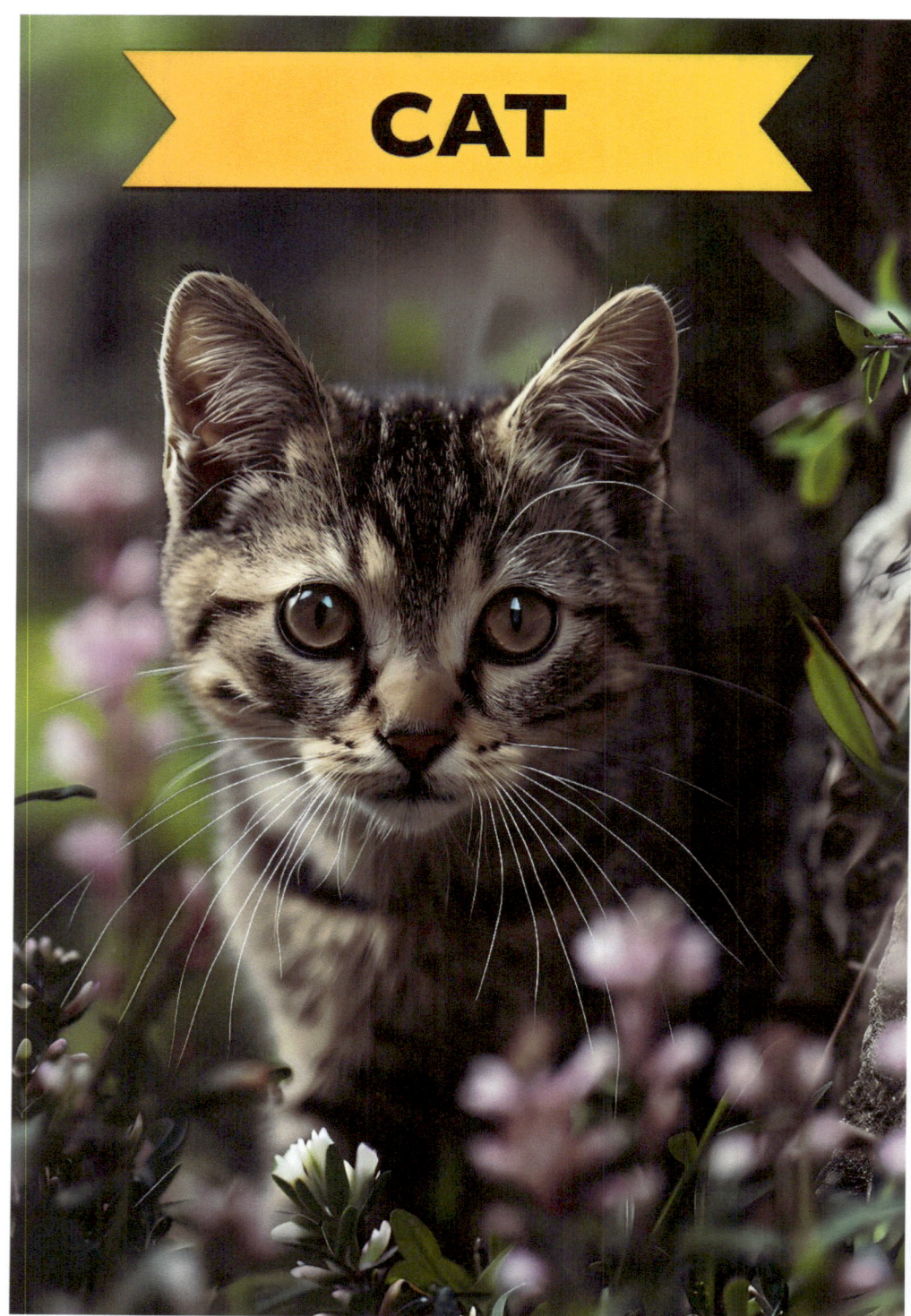

# CAT

# DOG

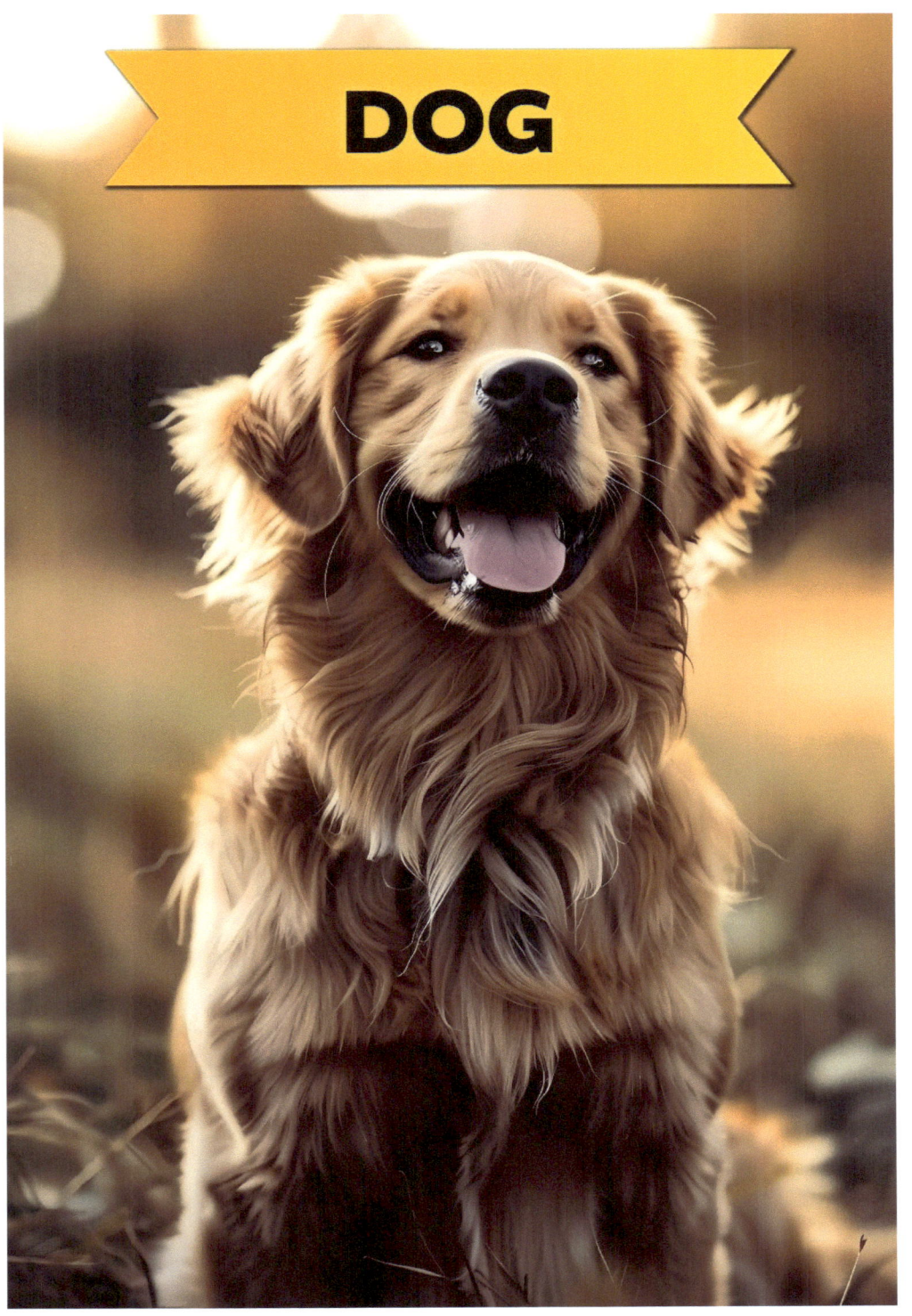

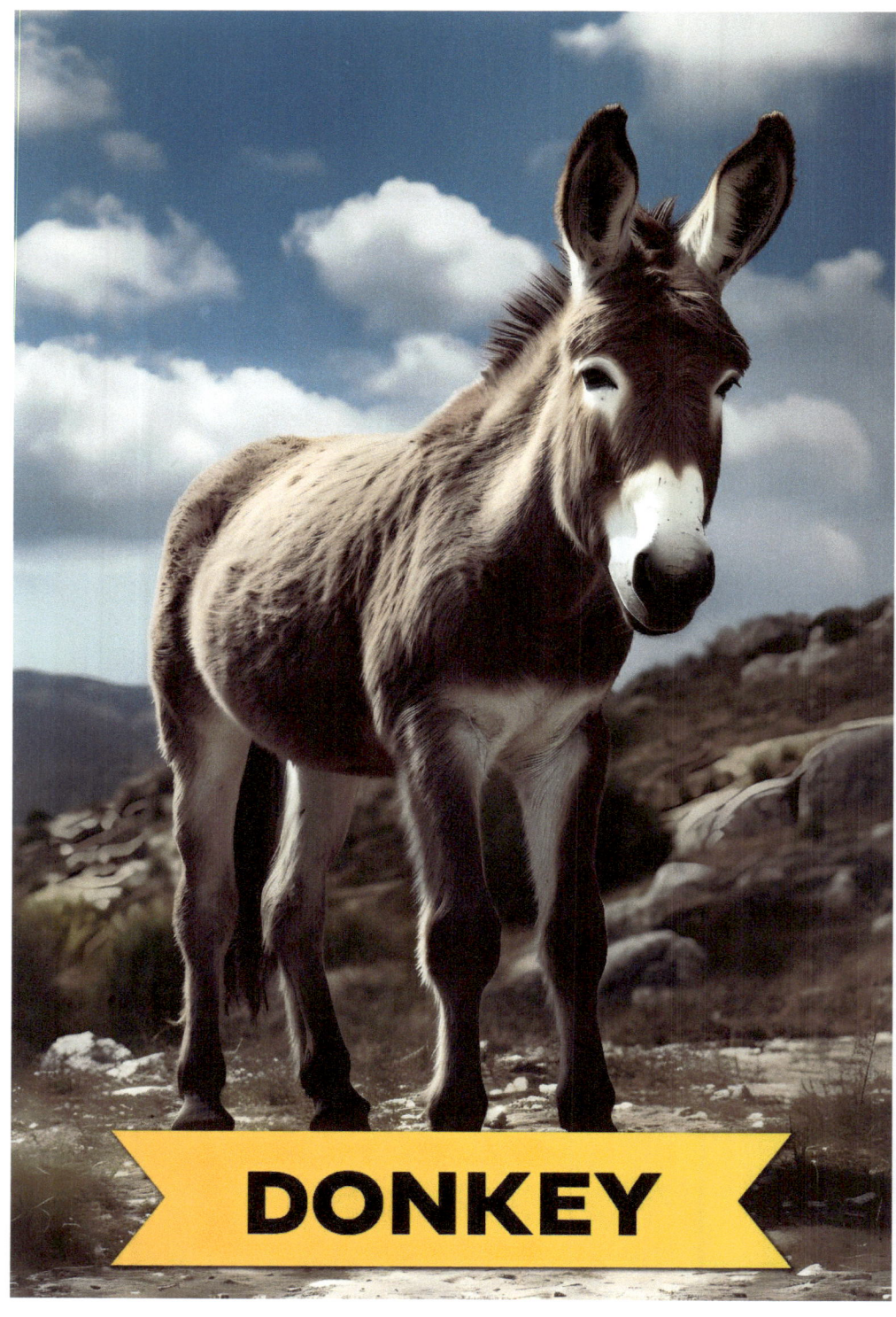

**DONKEY**

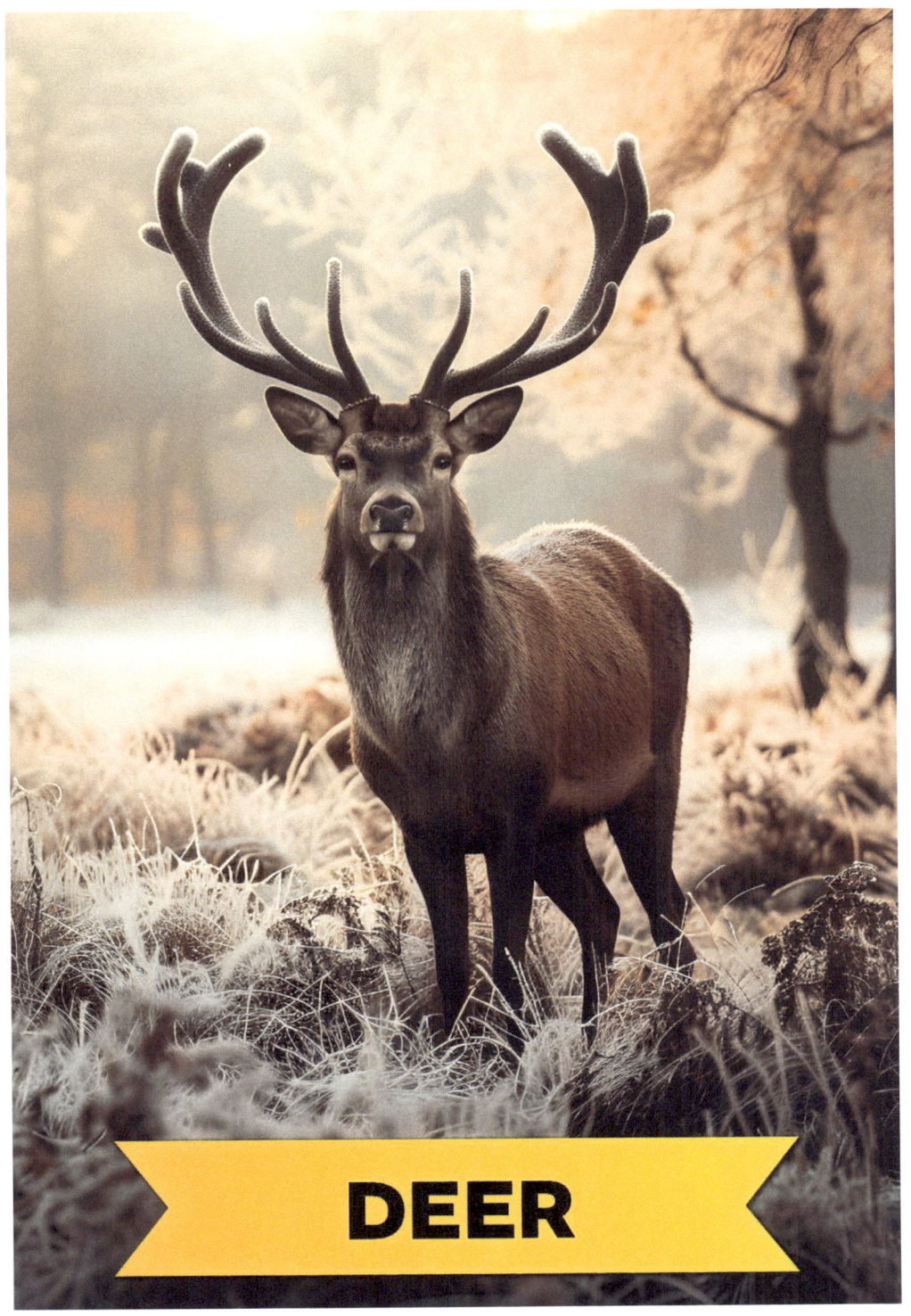

**DEER**

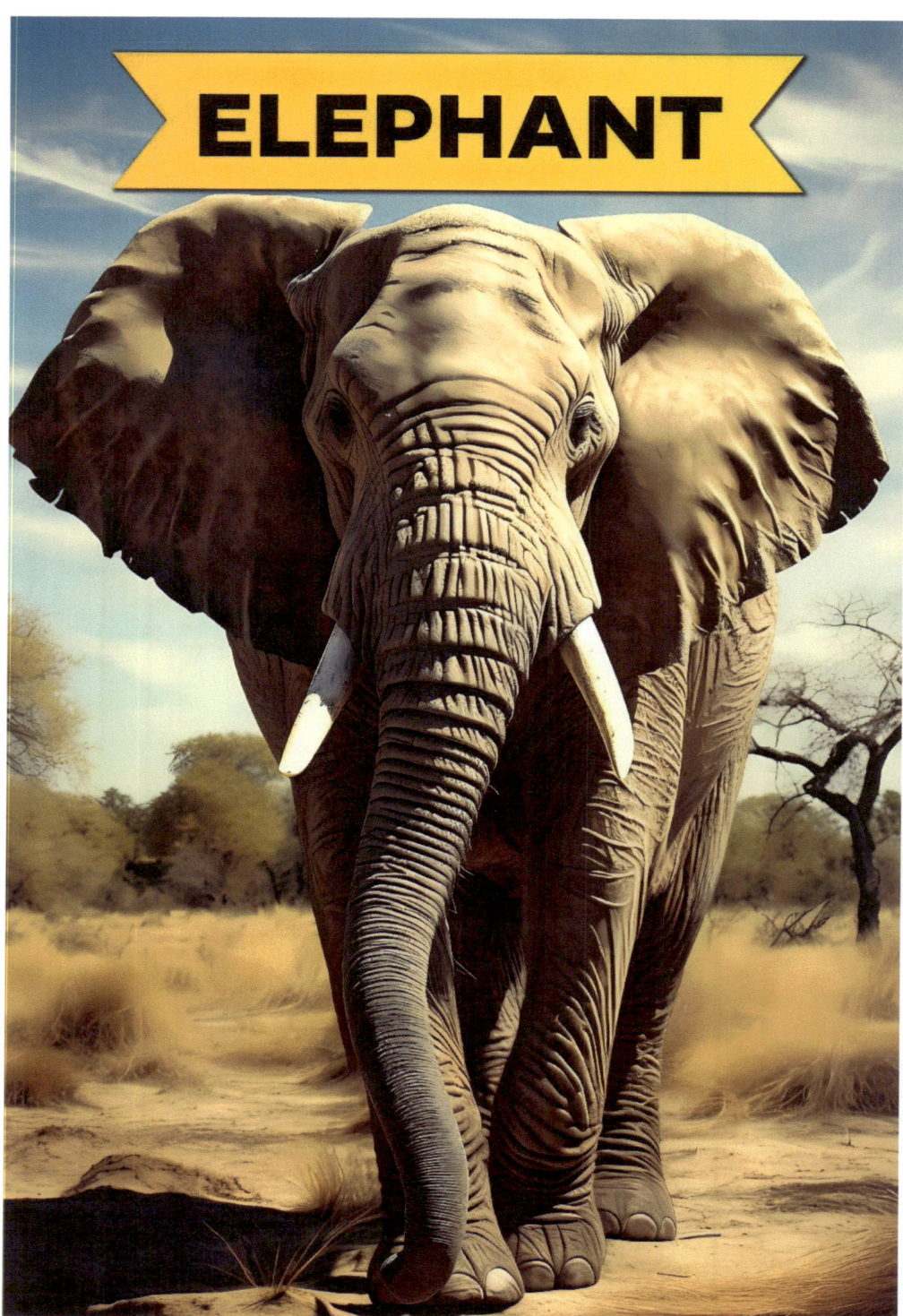

# FOX

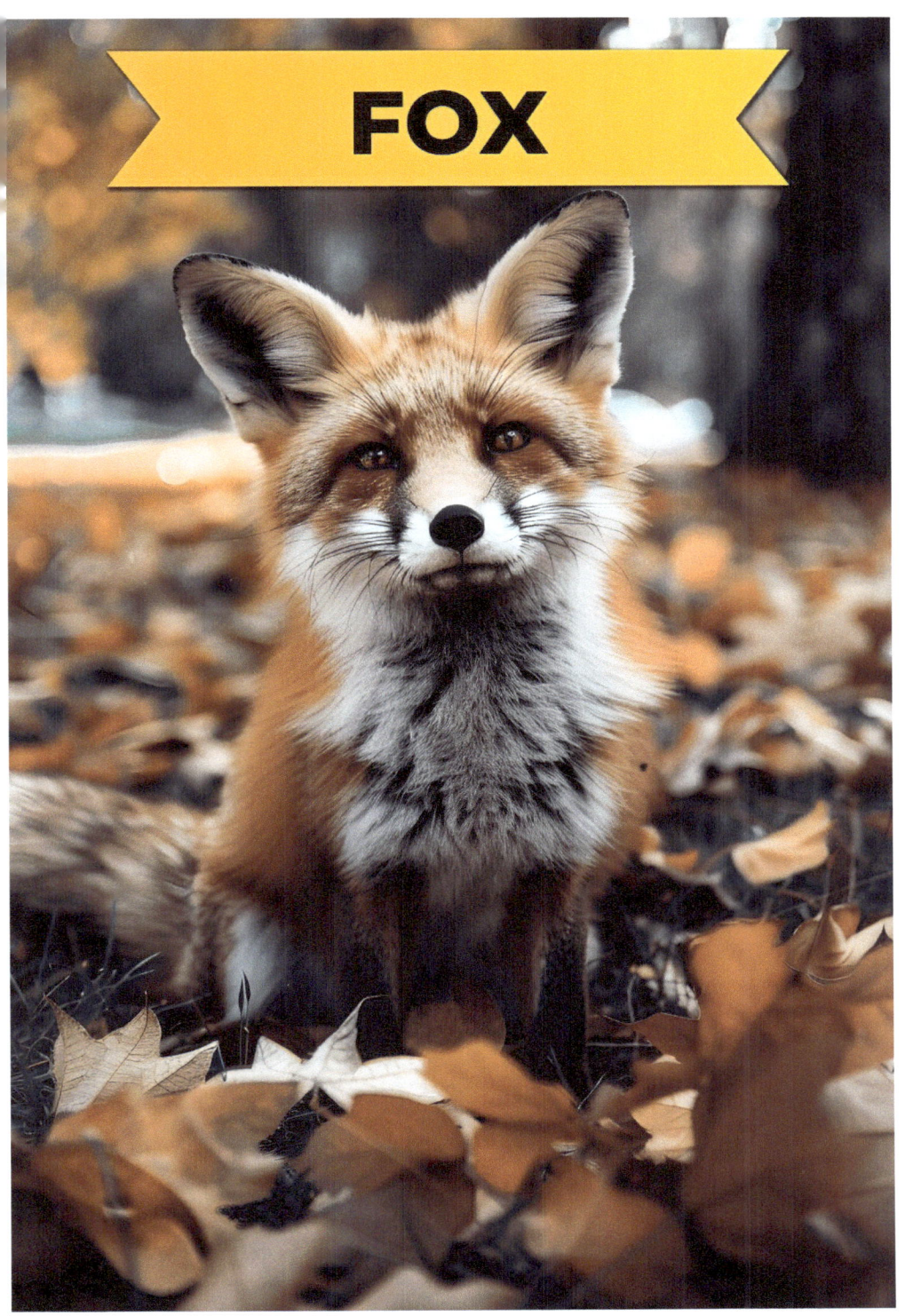

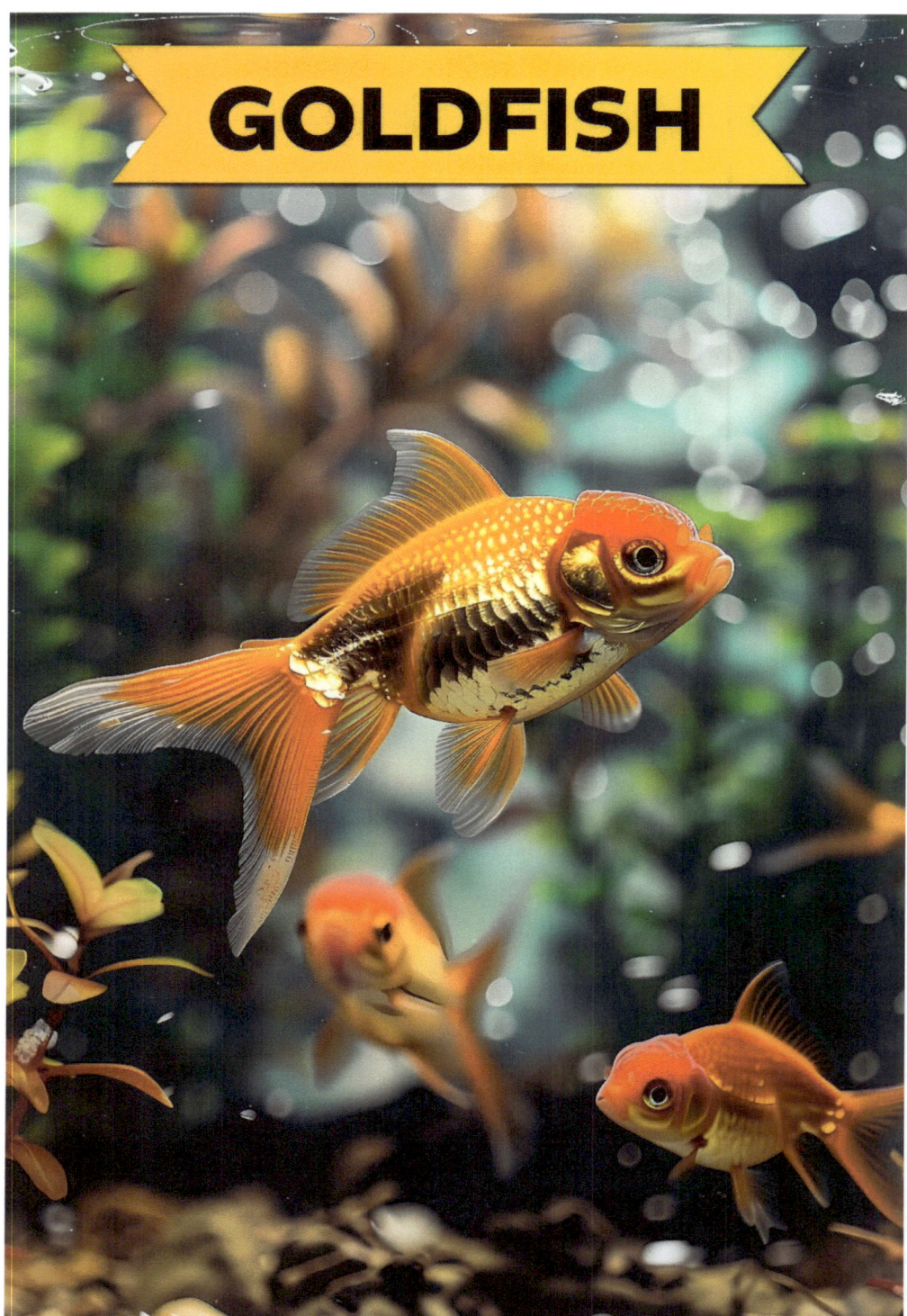

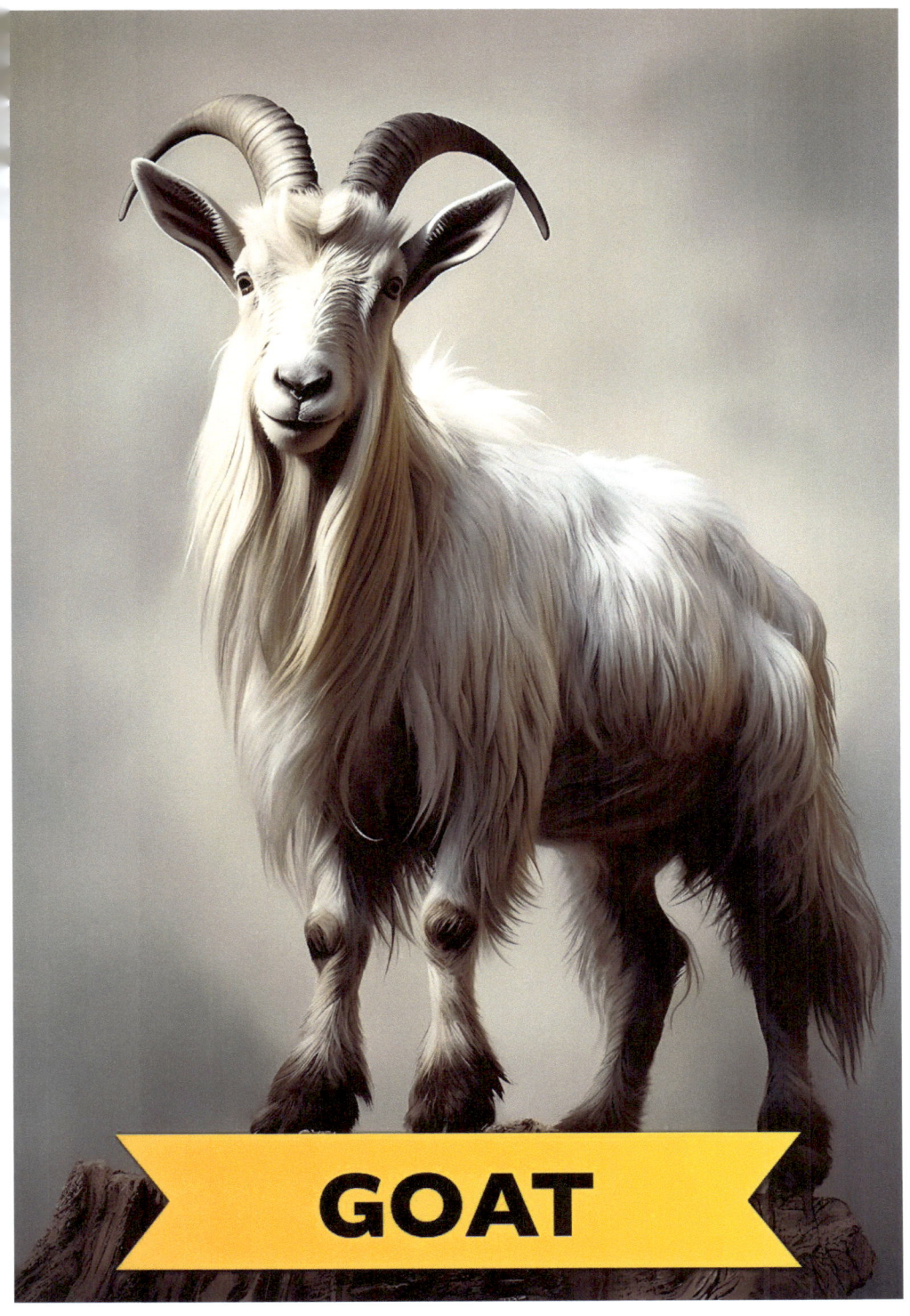

GOAT

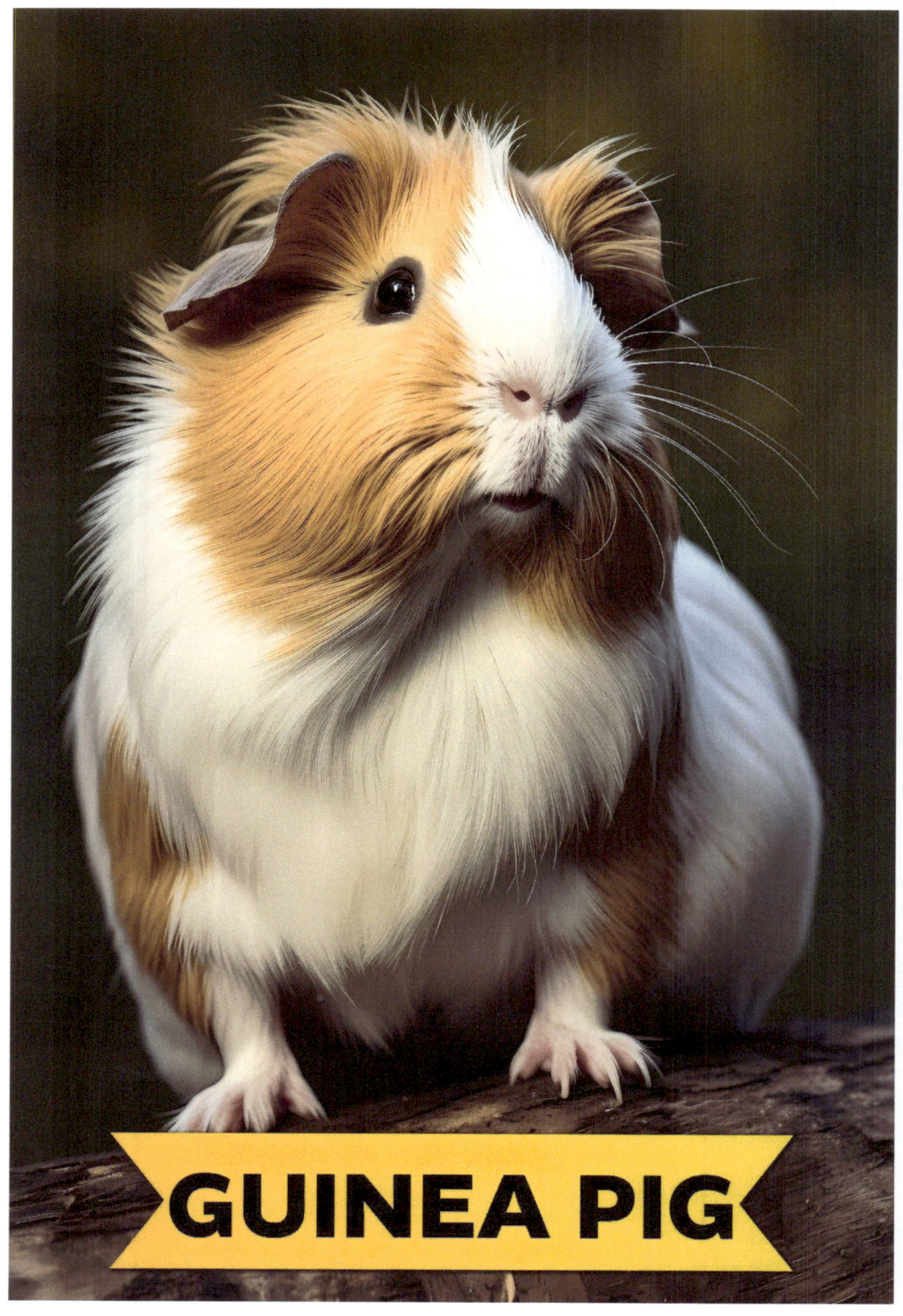

**GUINEA PIG**

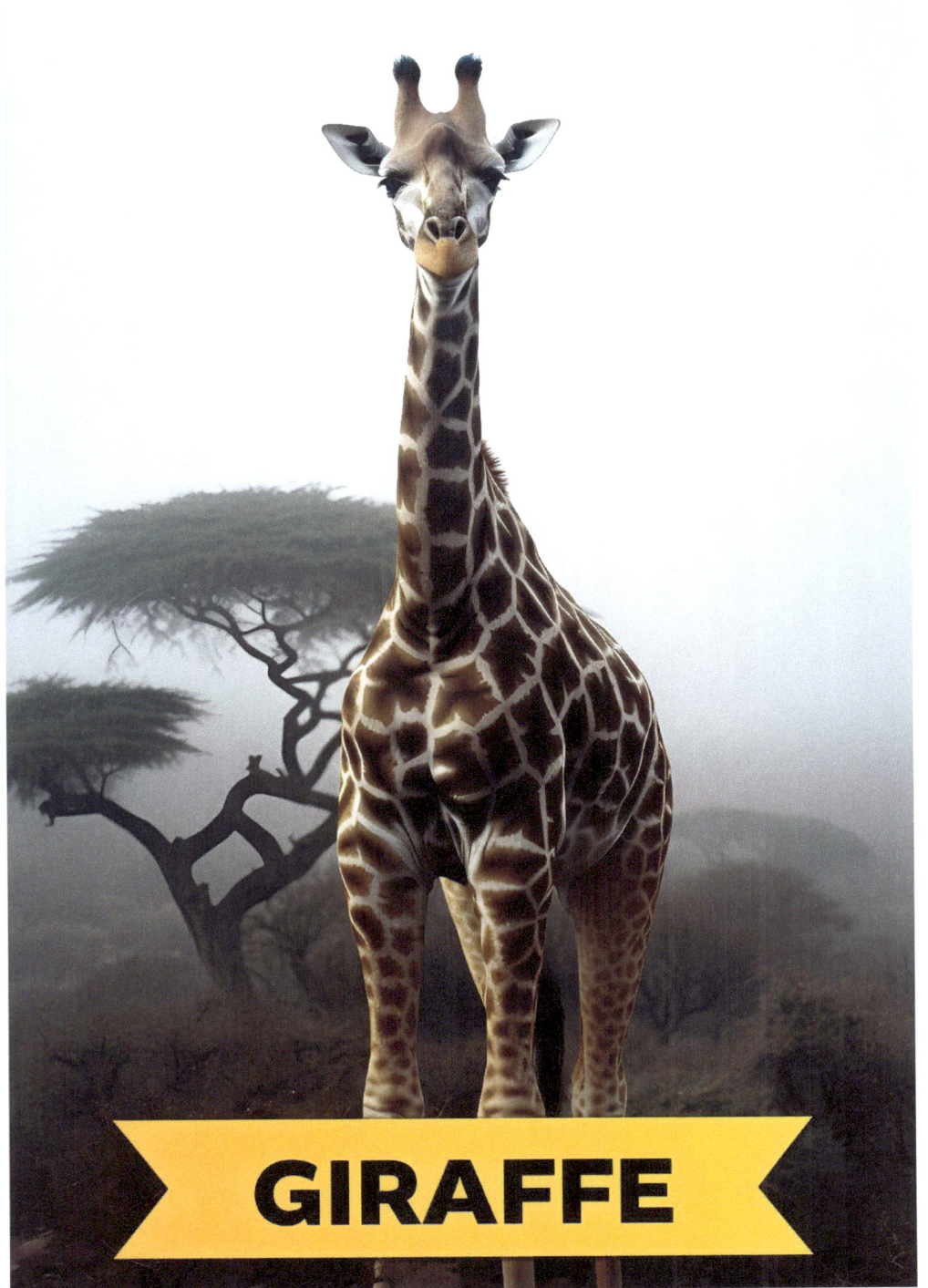

**GIRAFFE**

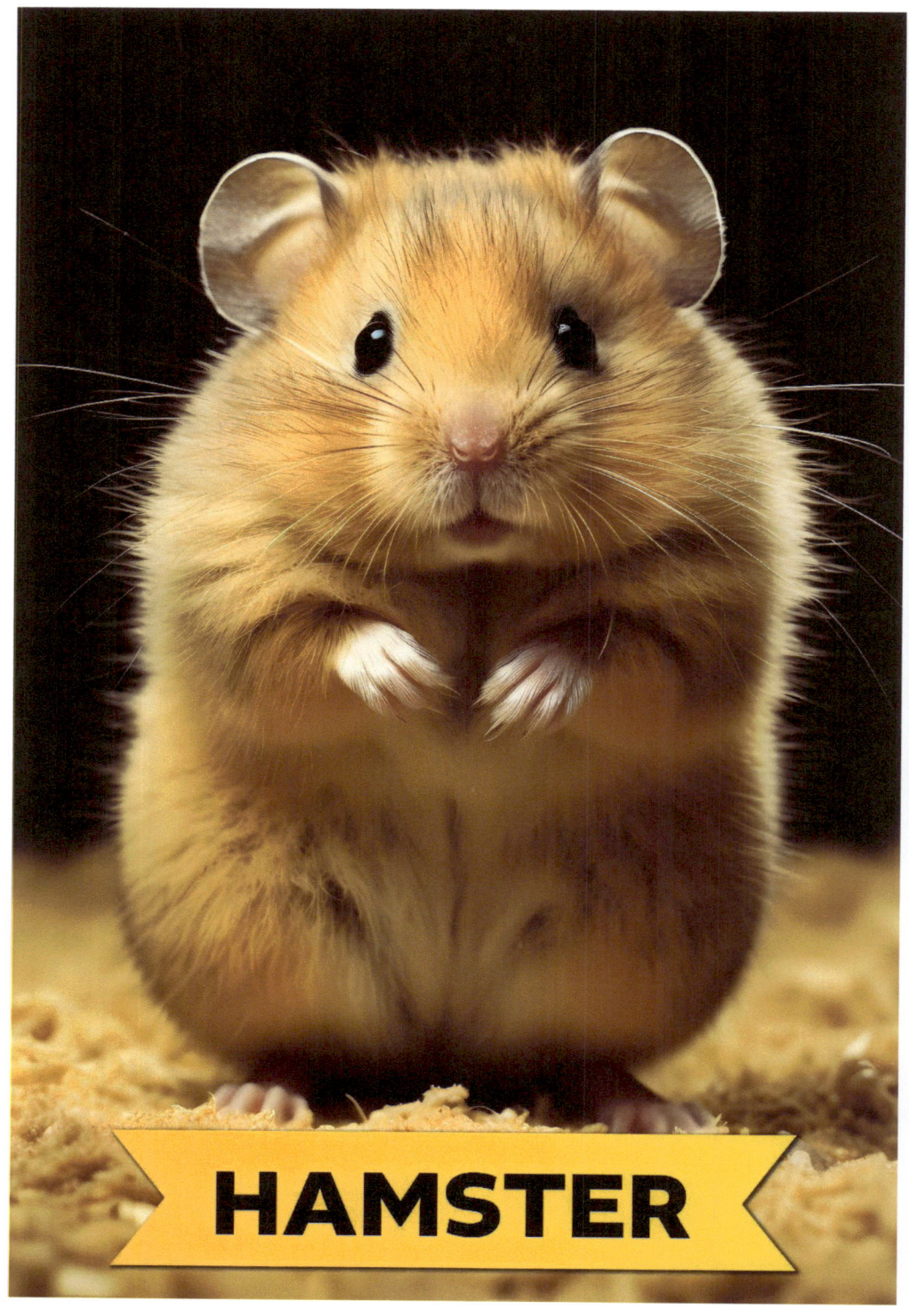

**HAMSTER**

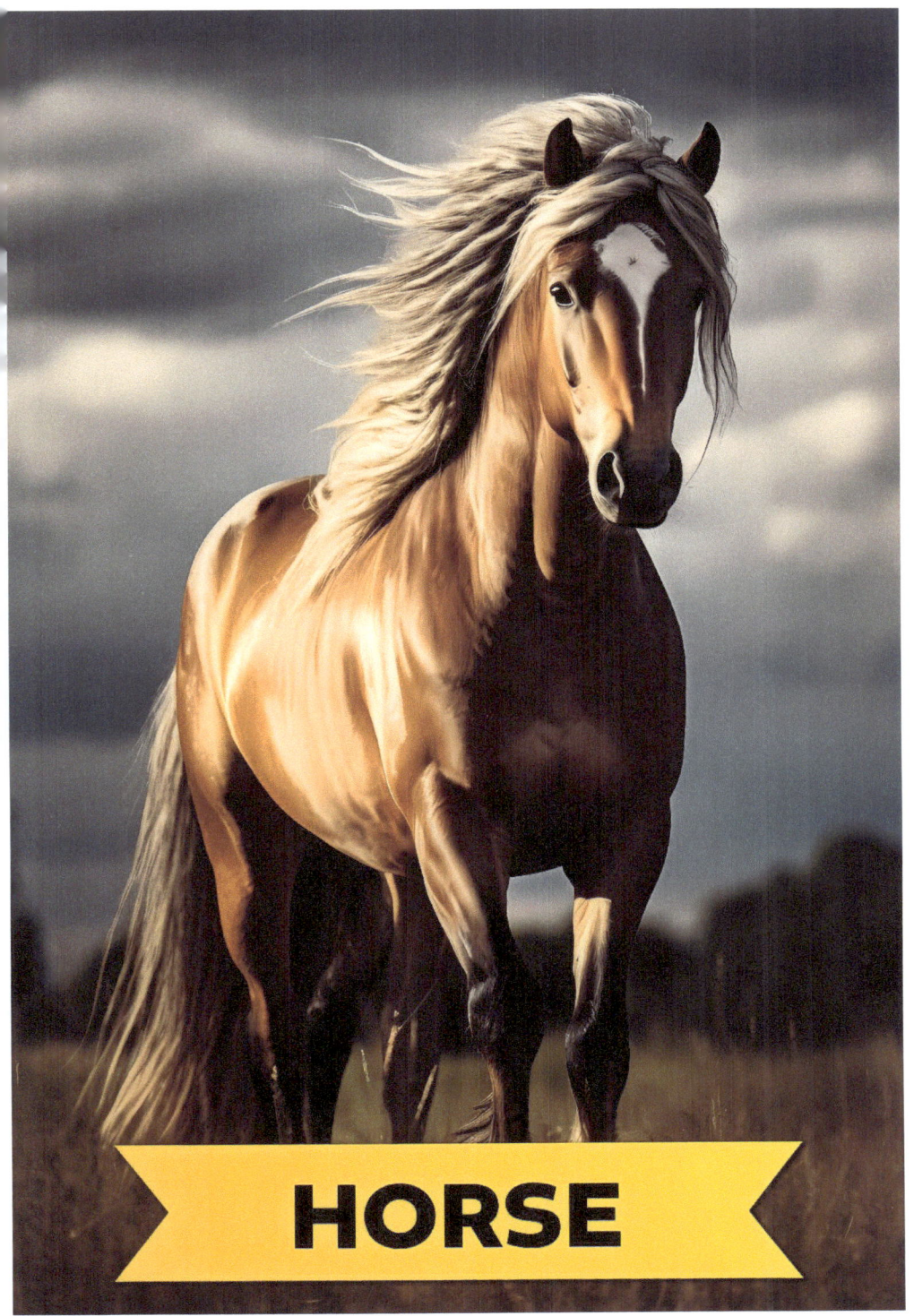

**HORSE**

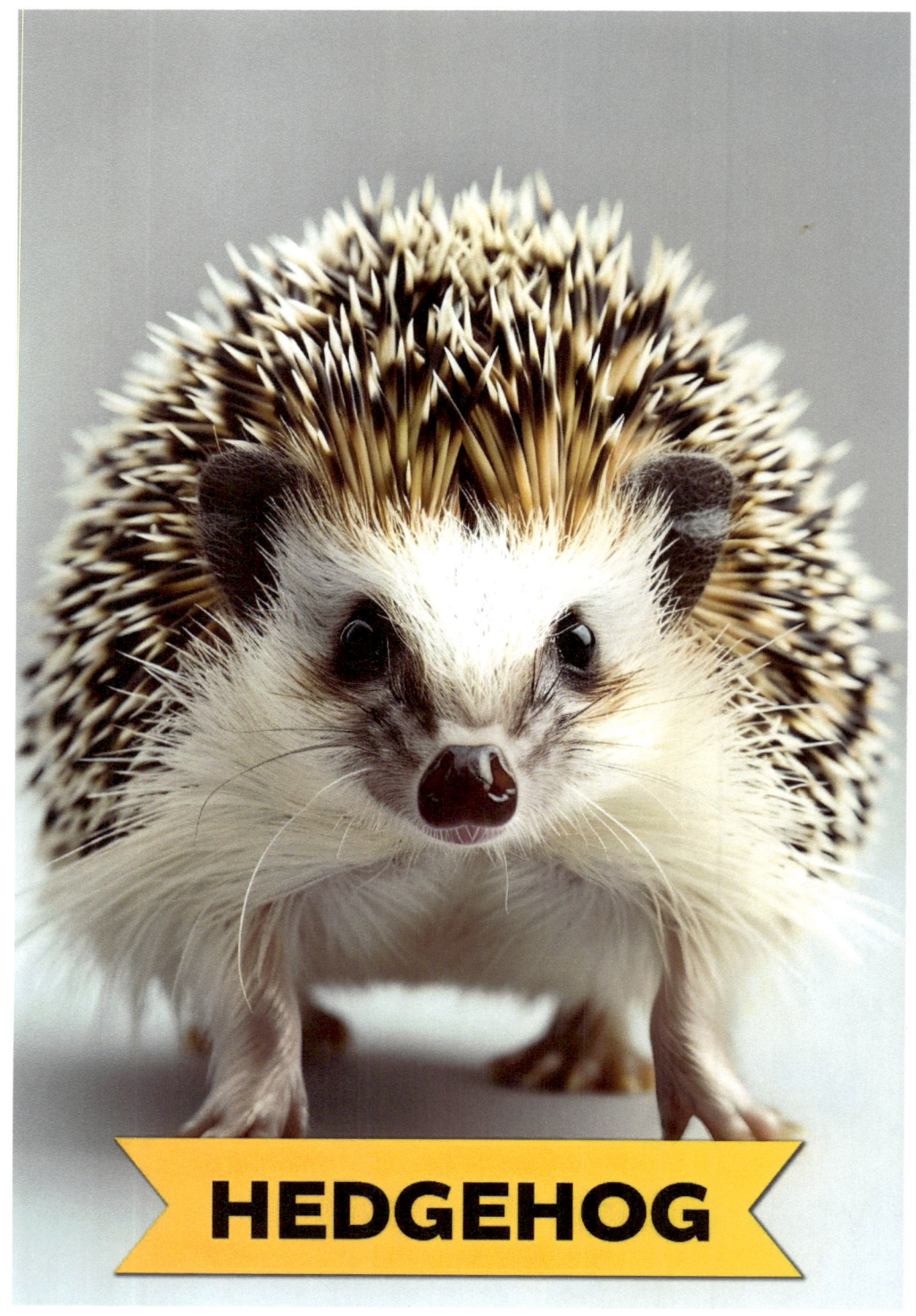

**HEDGEHOG**

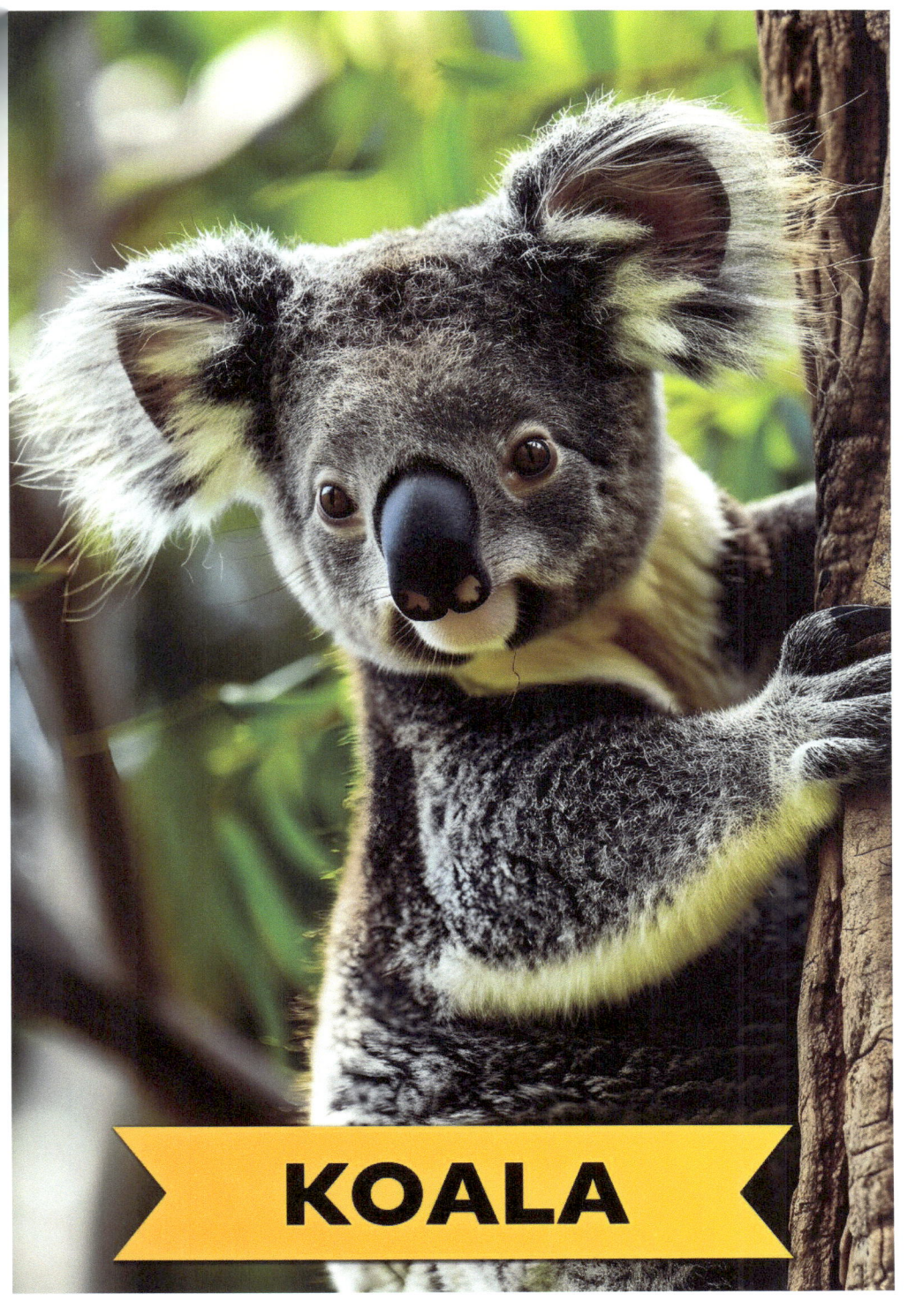

**KOALA**

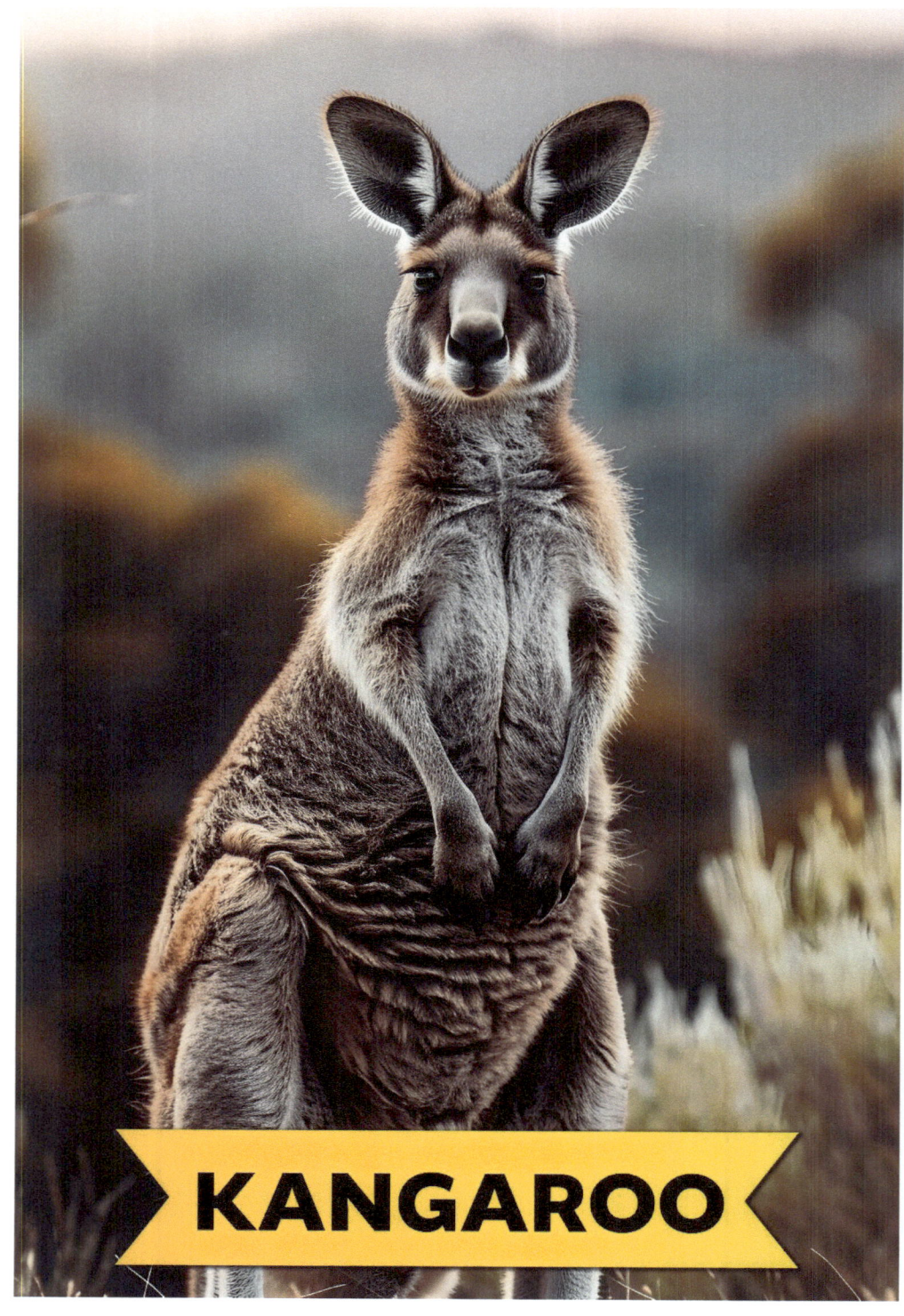

**KANGAROO**

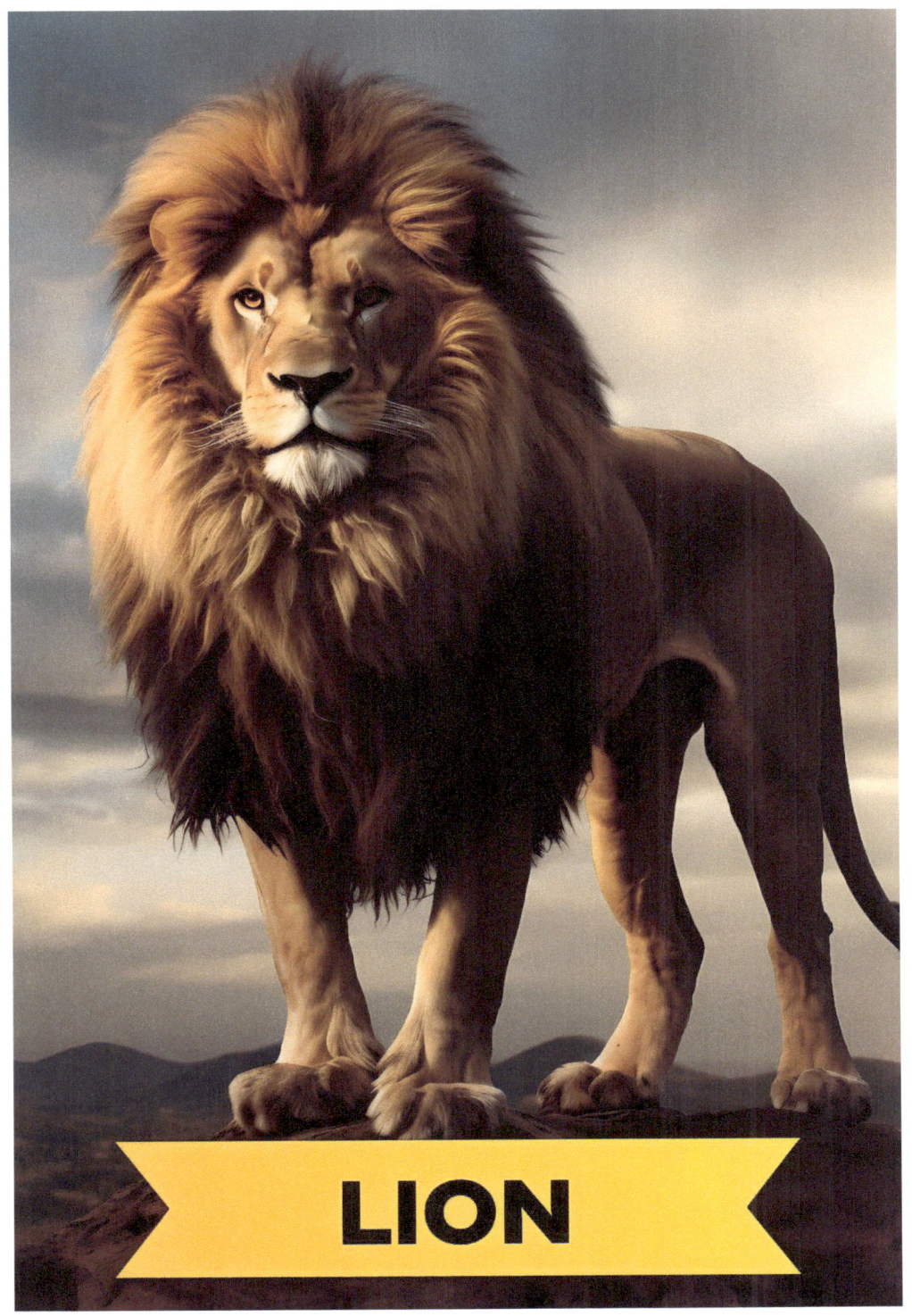

**LION**

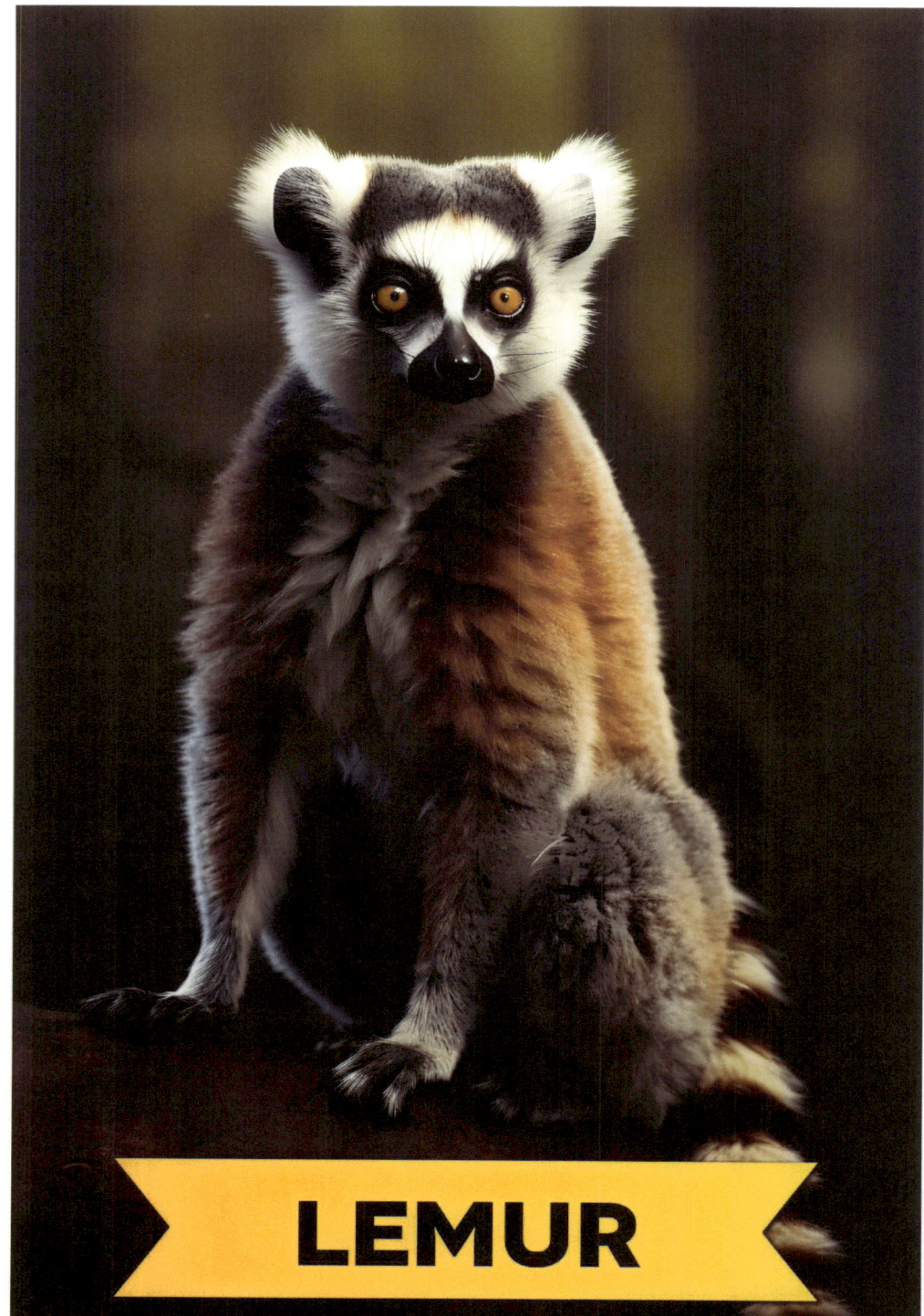

## LEMUR

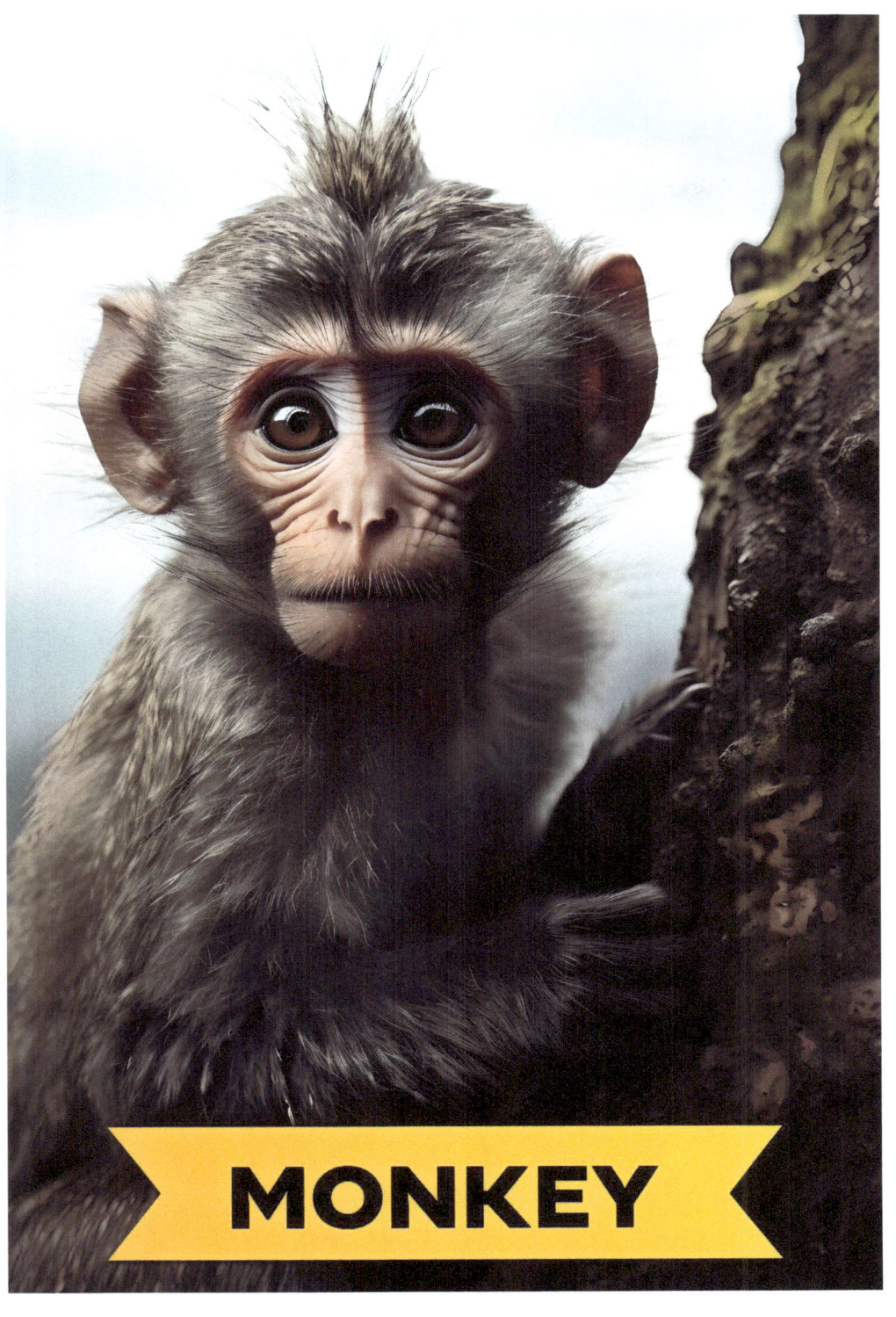

**MONKEY**

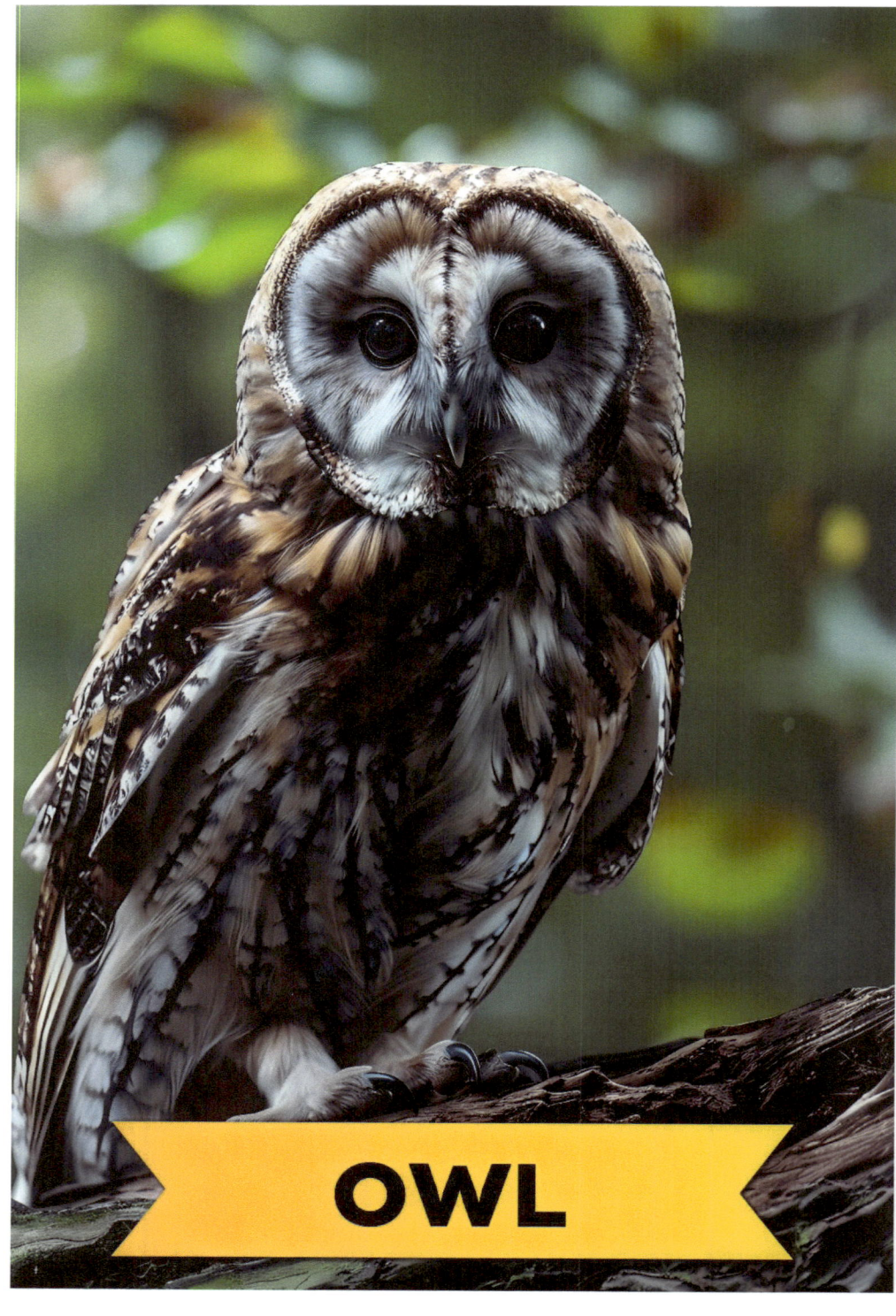

**OWL**

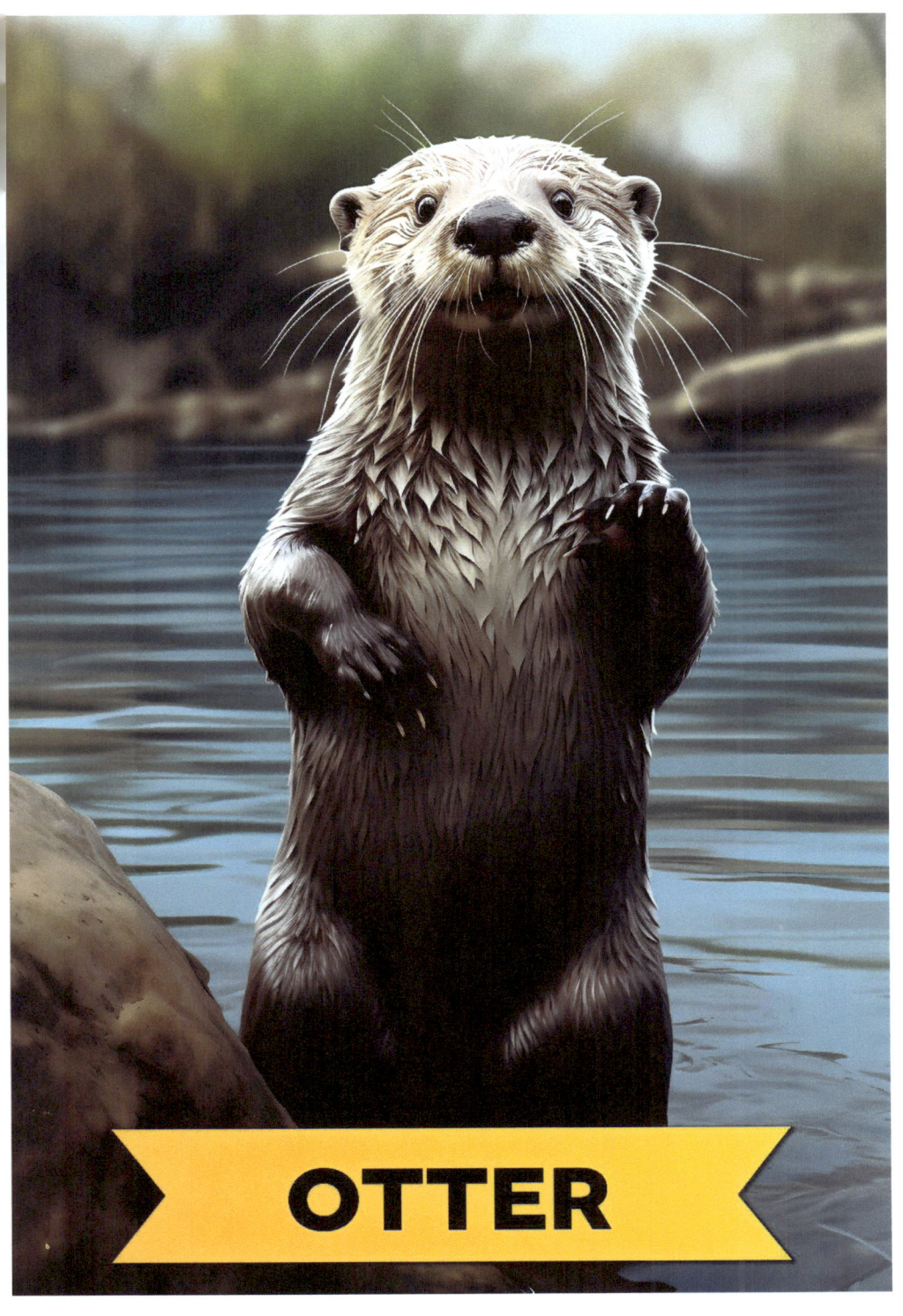

**OTTER**

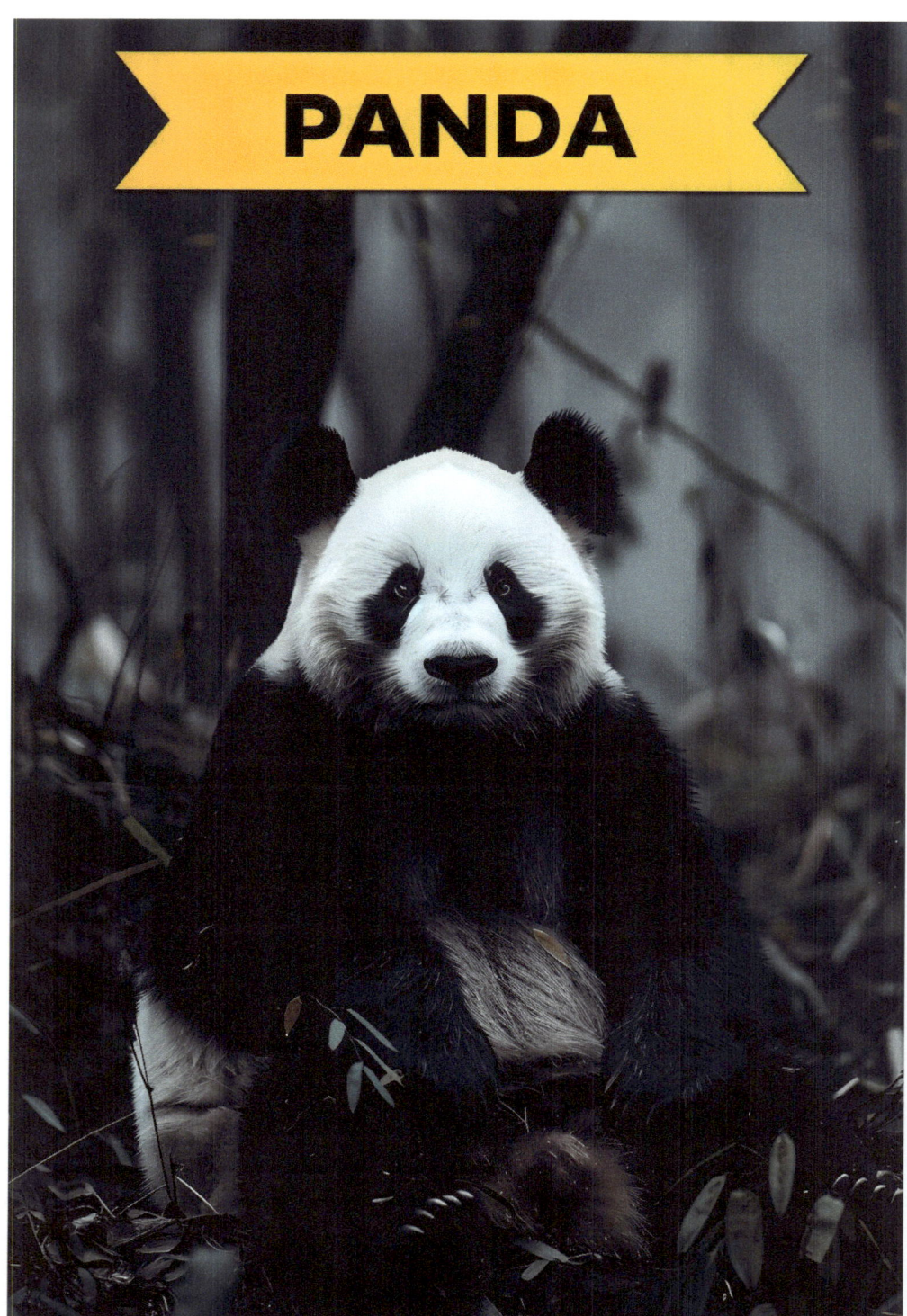

**PANDA**

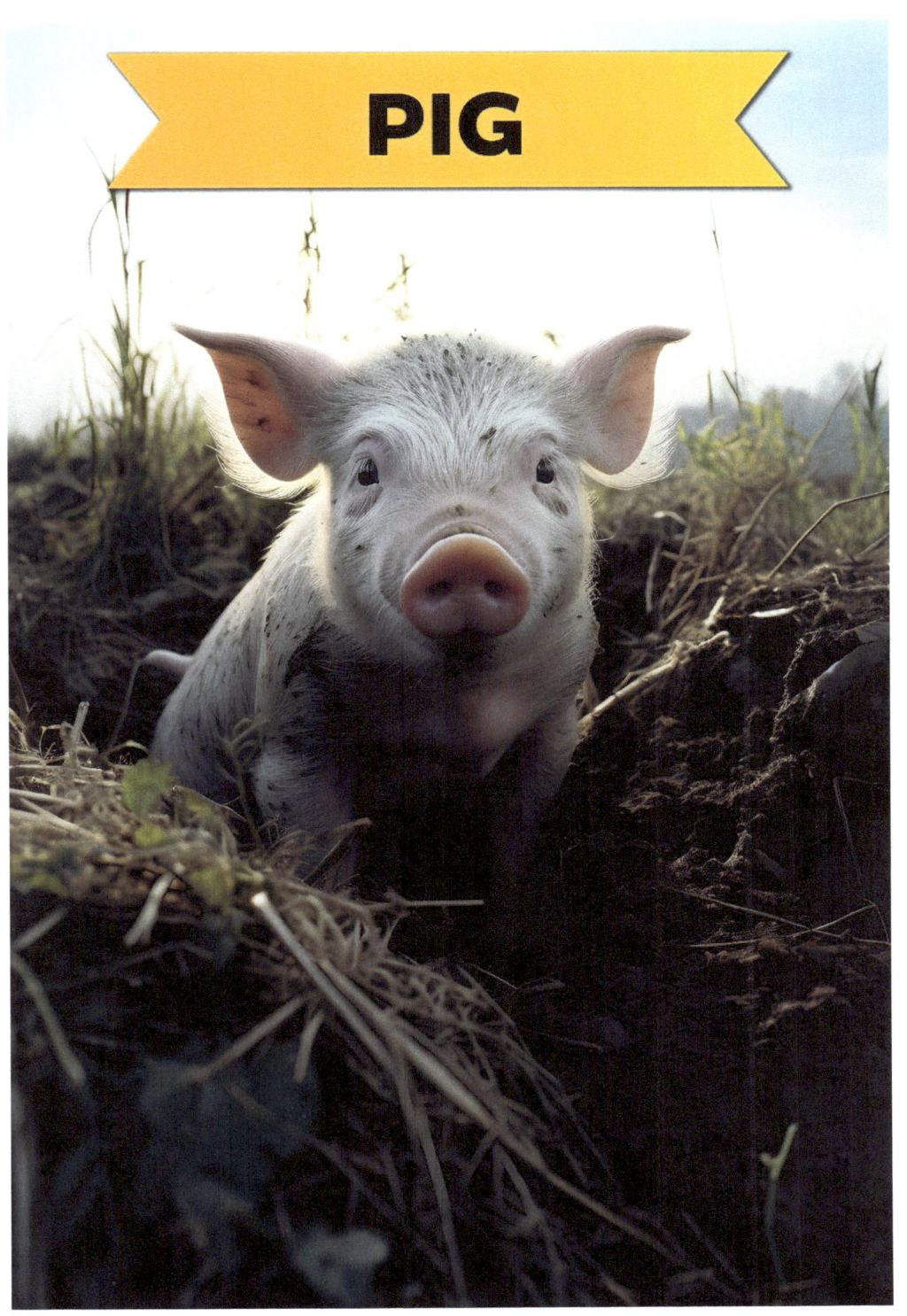

# PIG

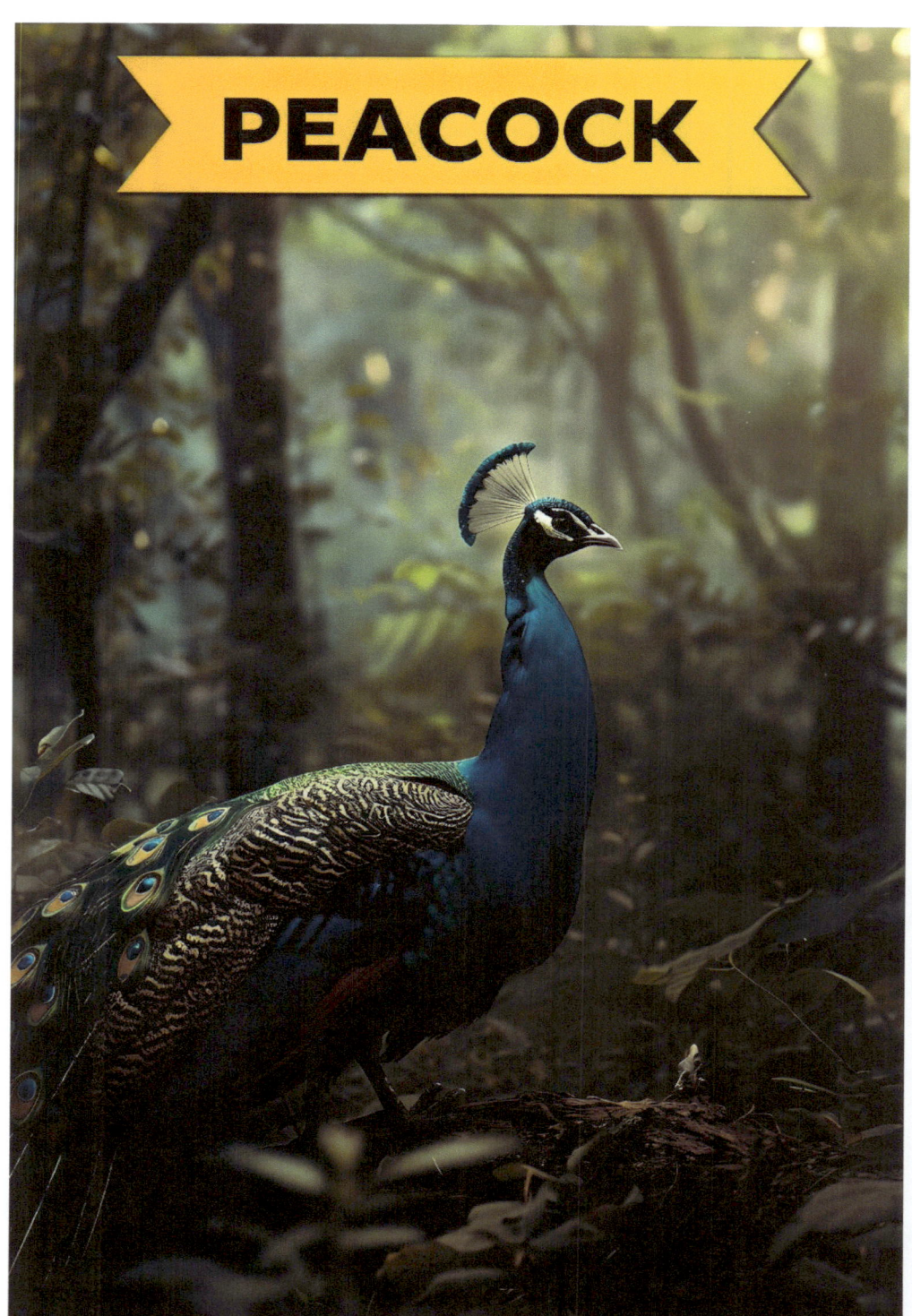

# PEACOCK

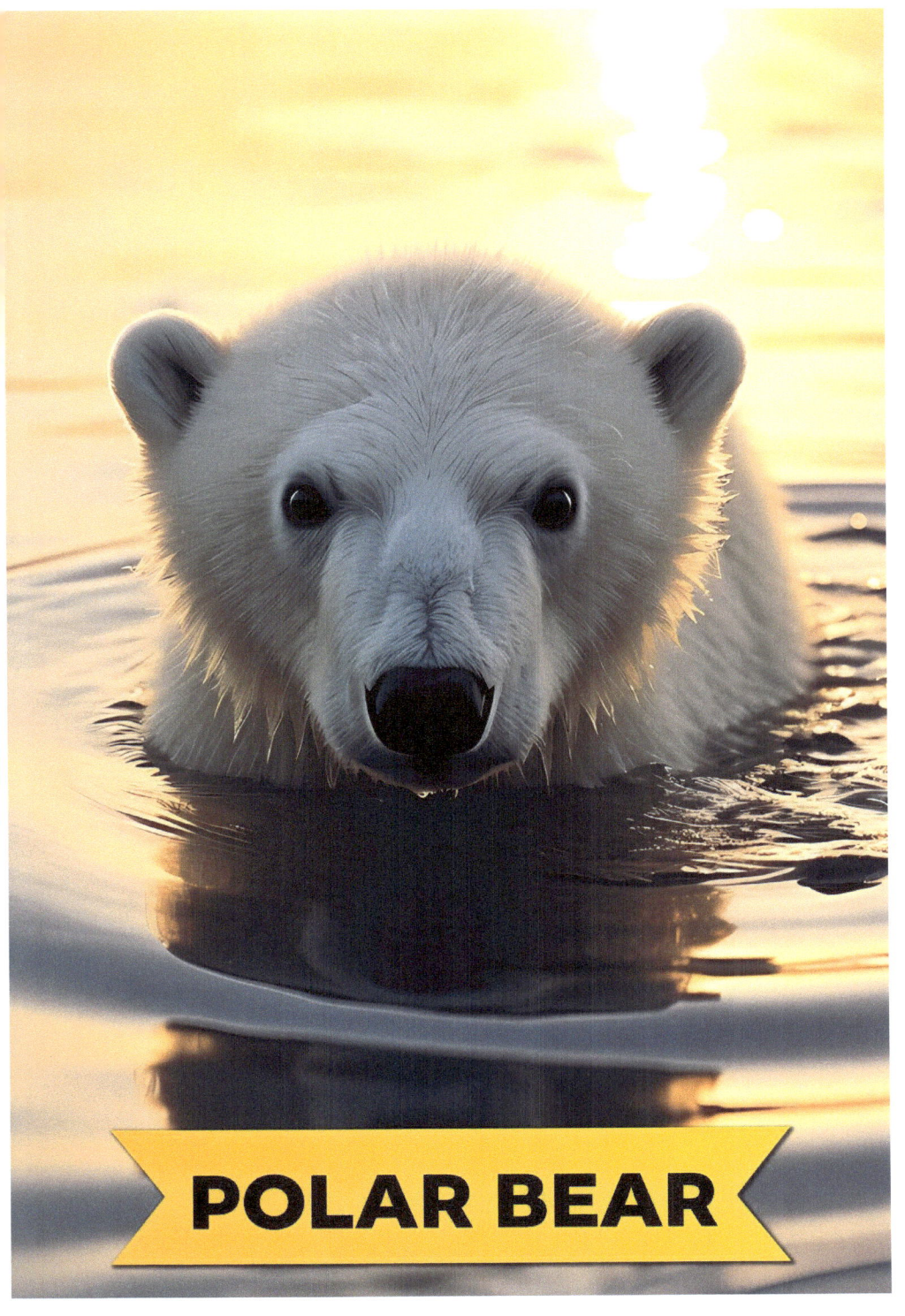

**POLAR BEAR**

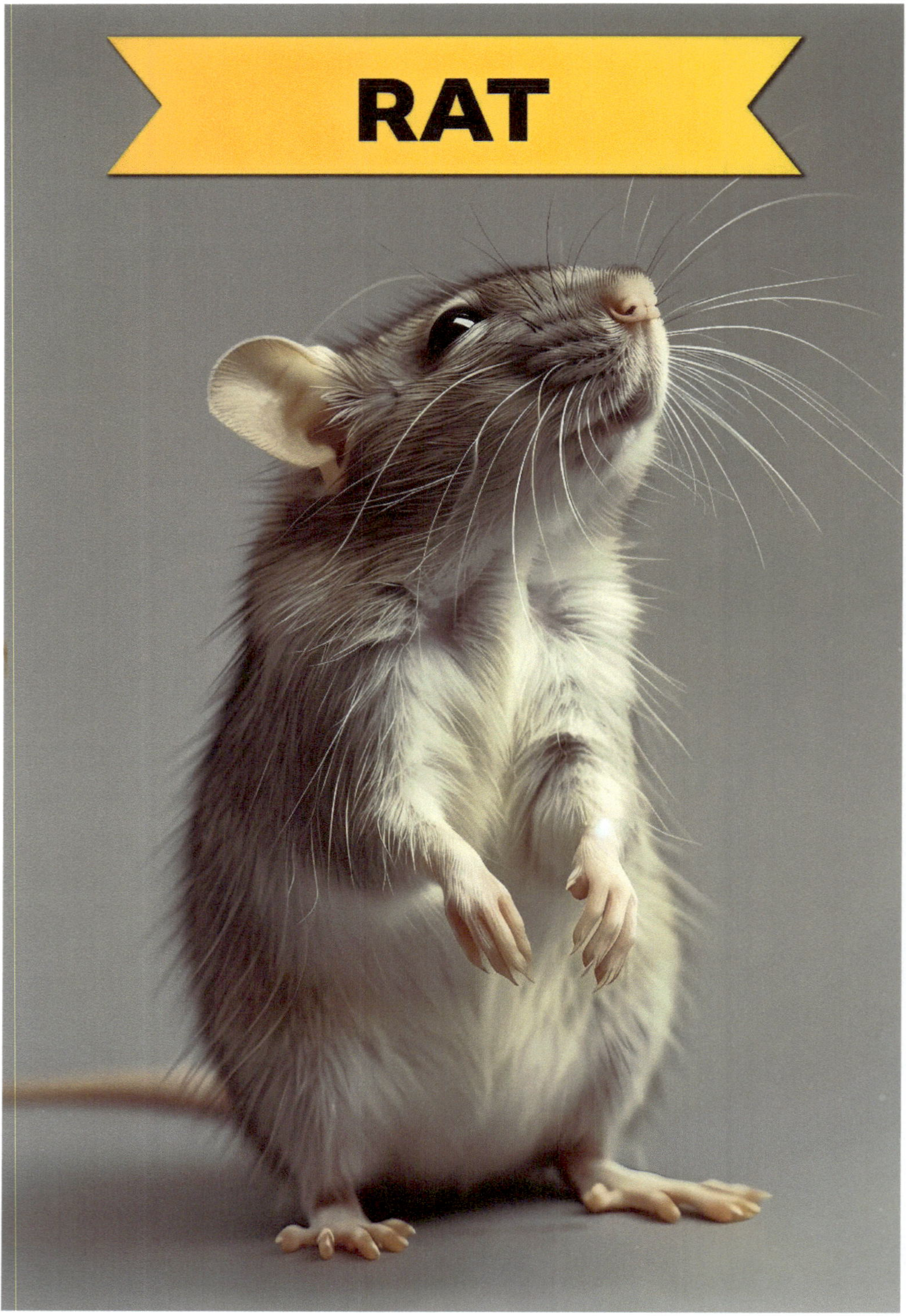

# RAT

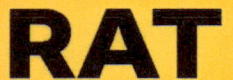

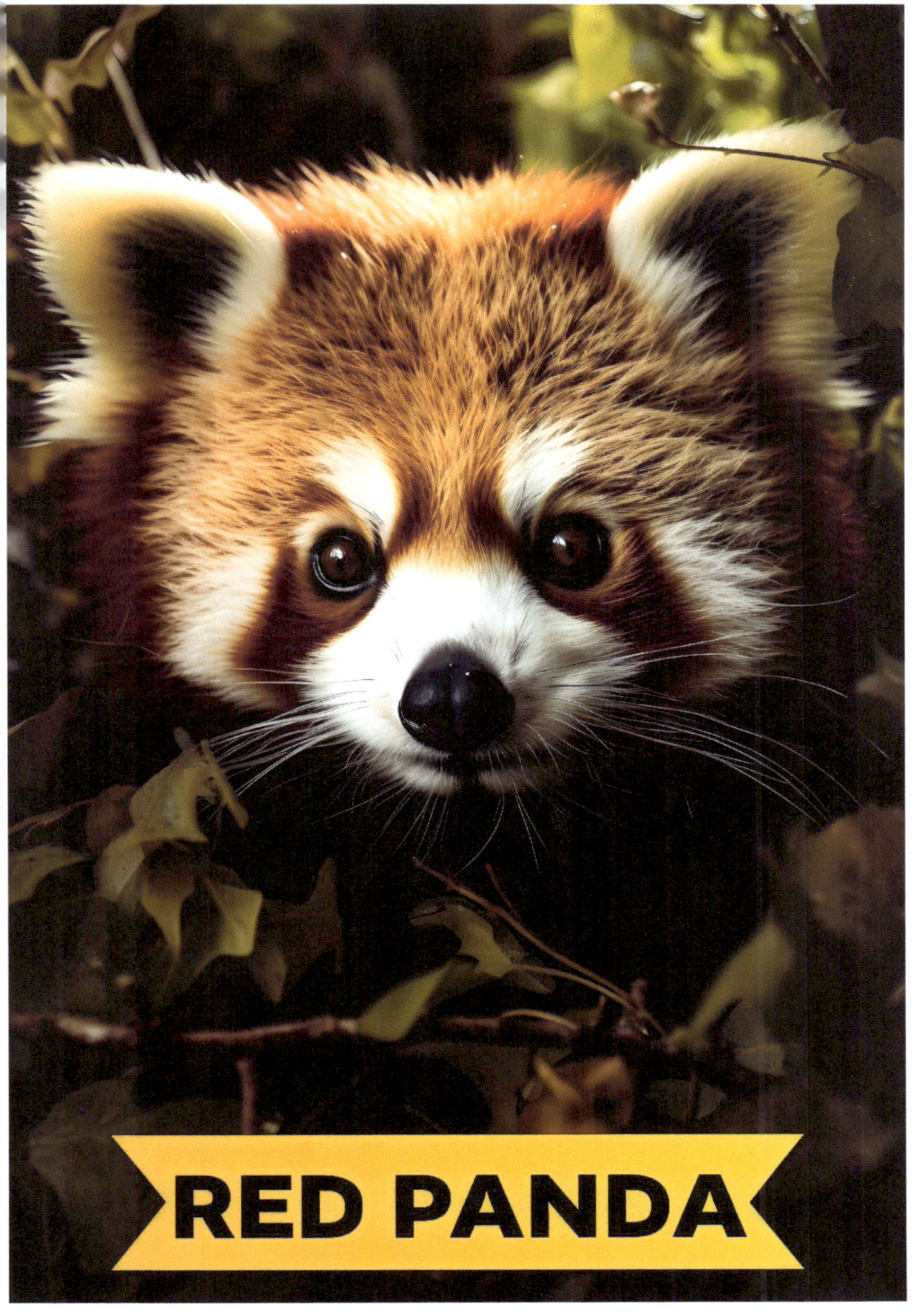

**RED PANDA**

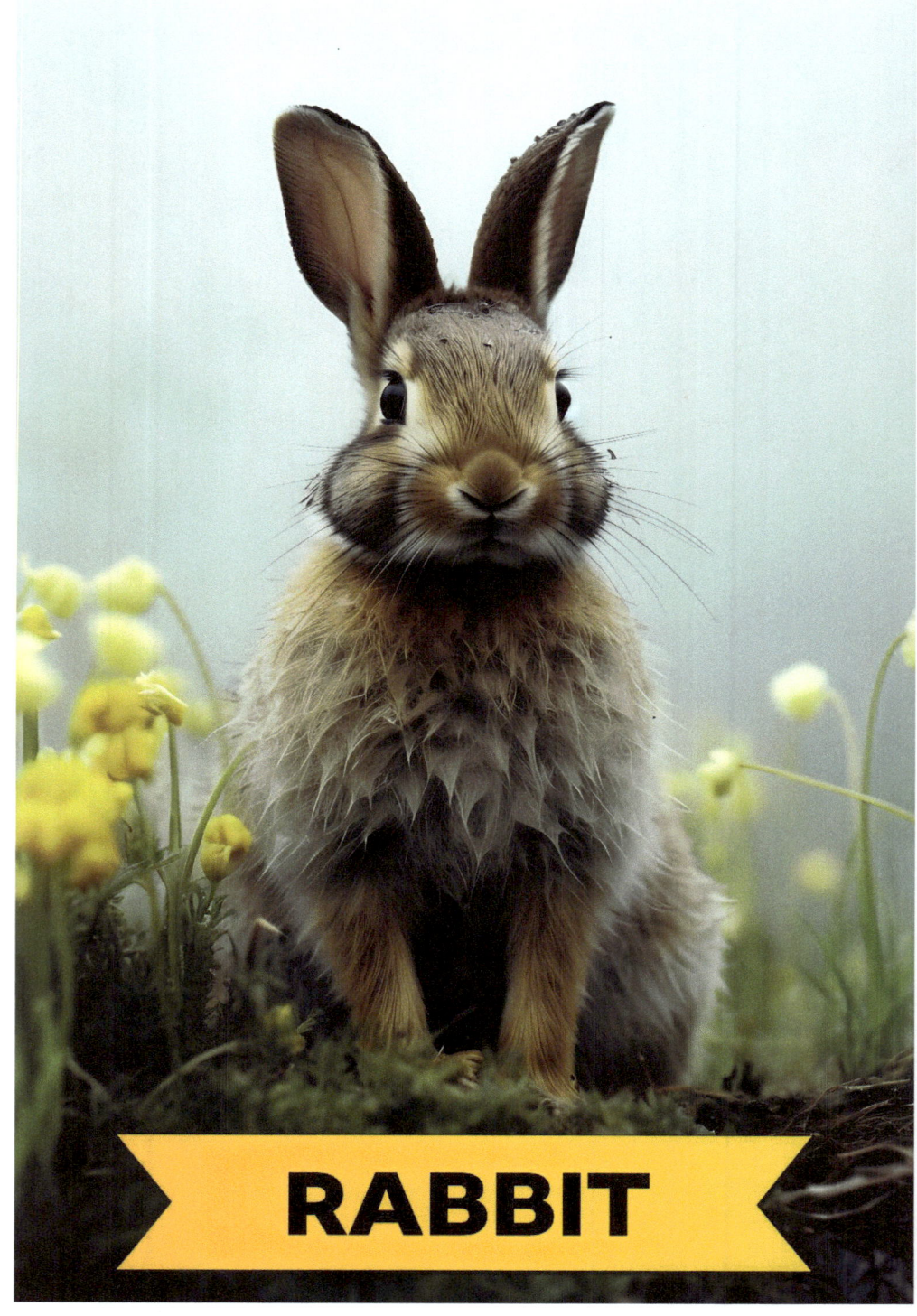

**RABBIT**

# SEA LION

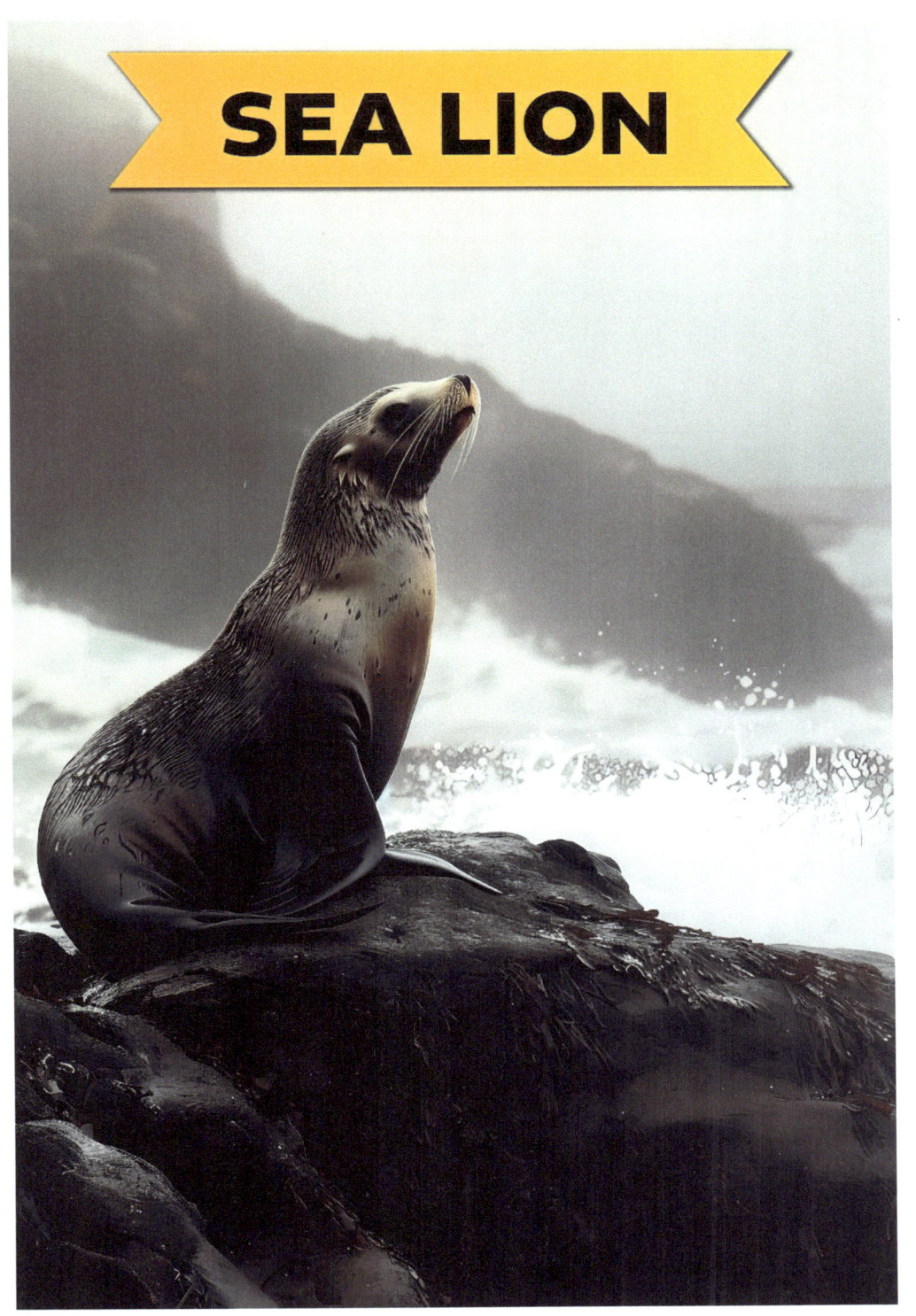

# SEAL

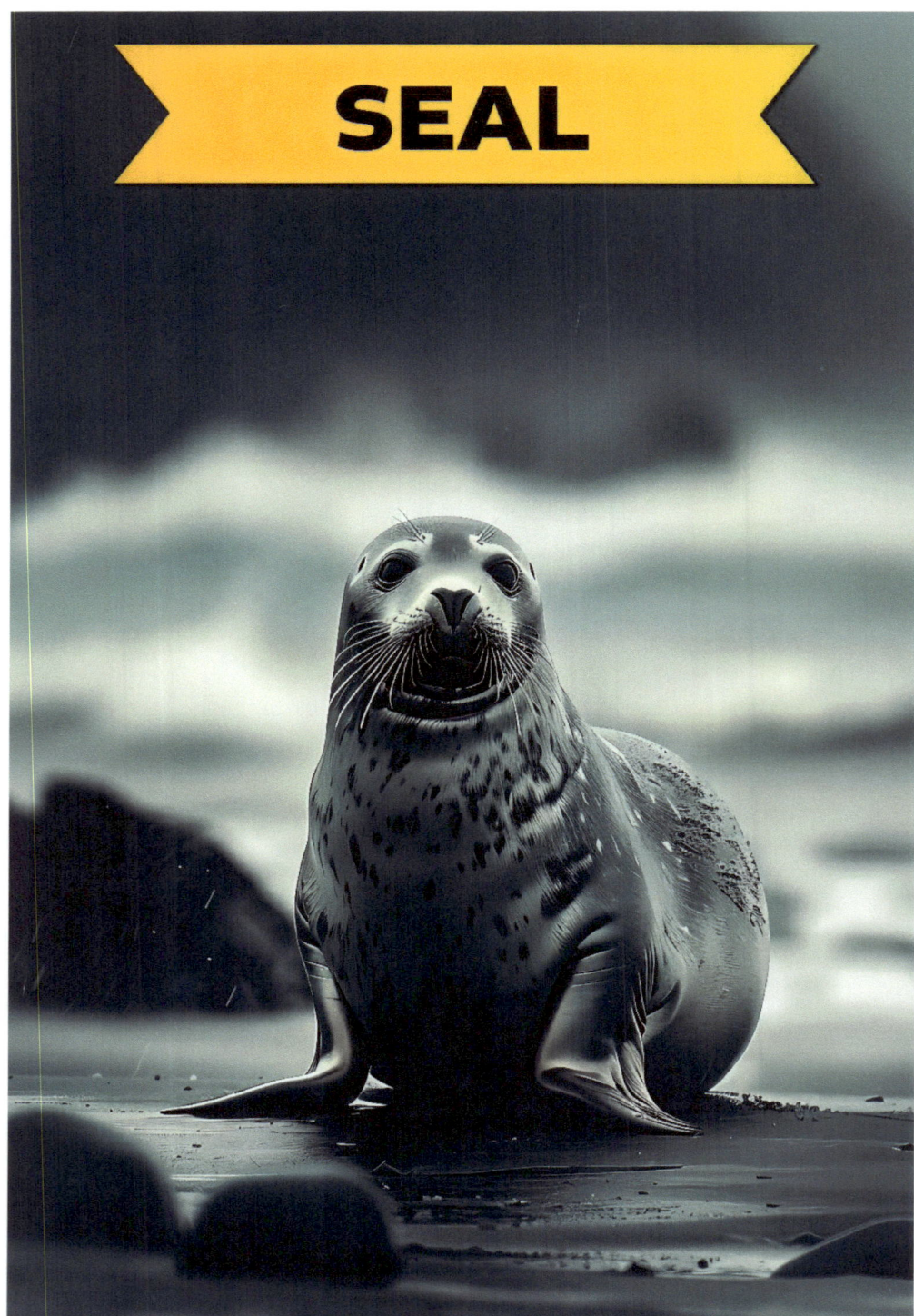

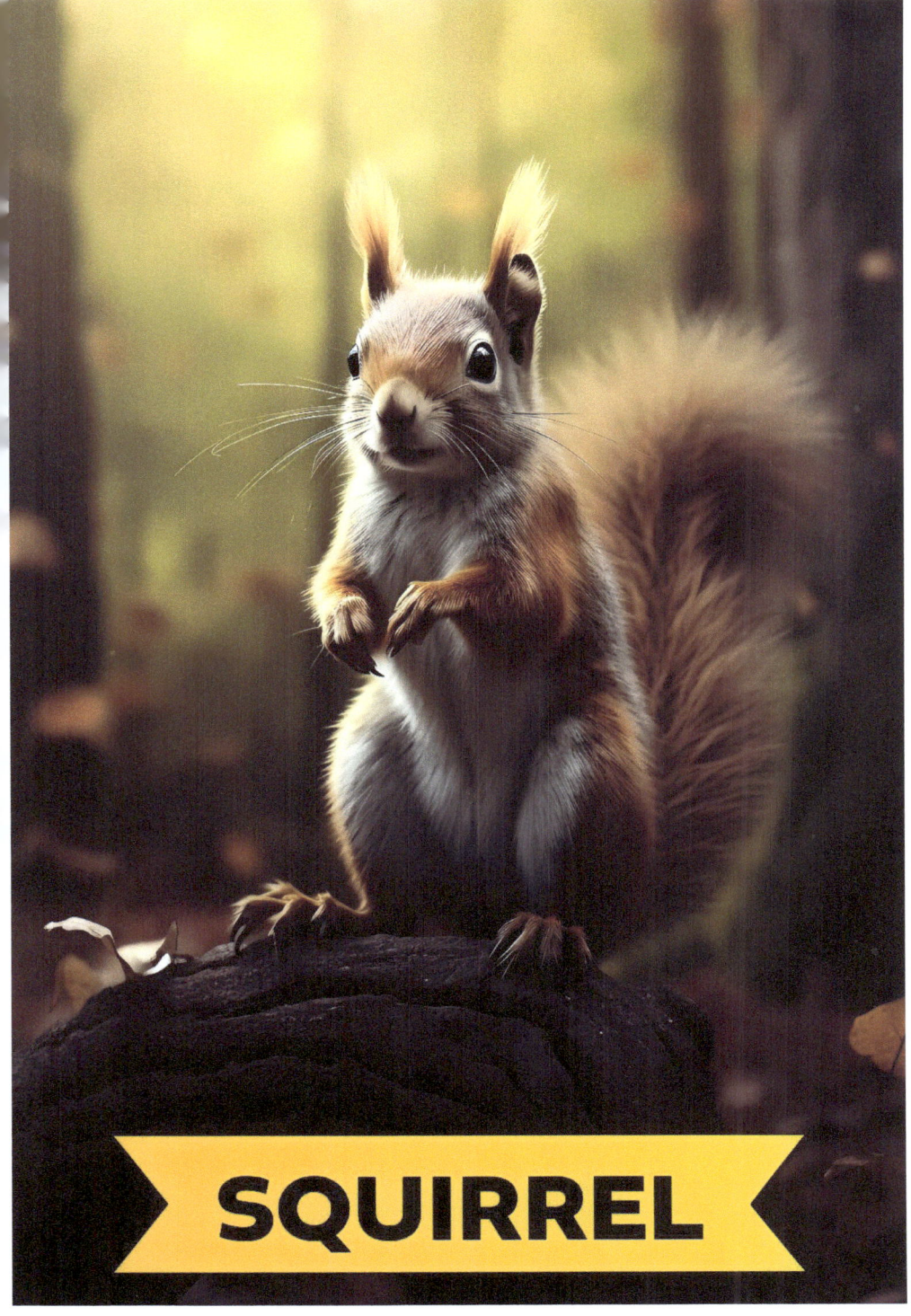

**SQUIRREL**

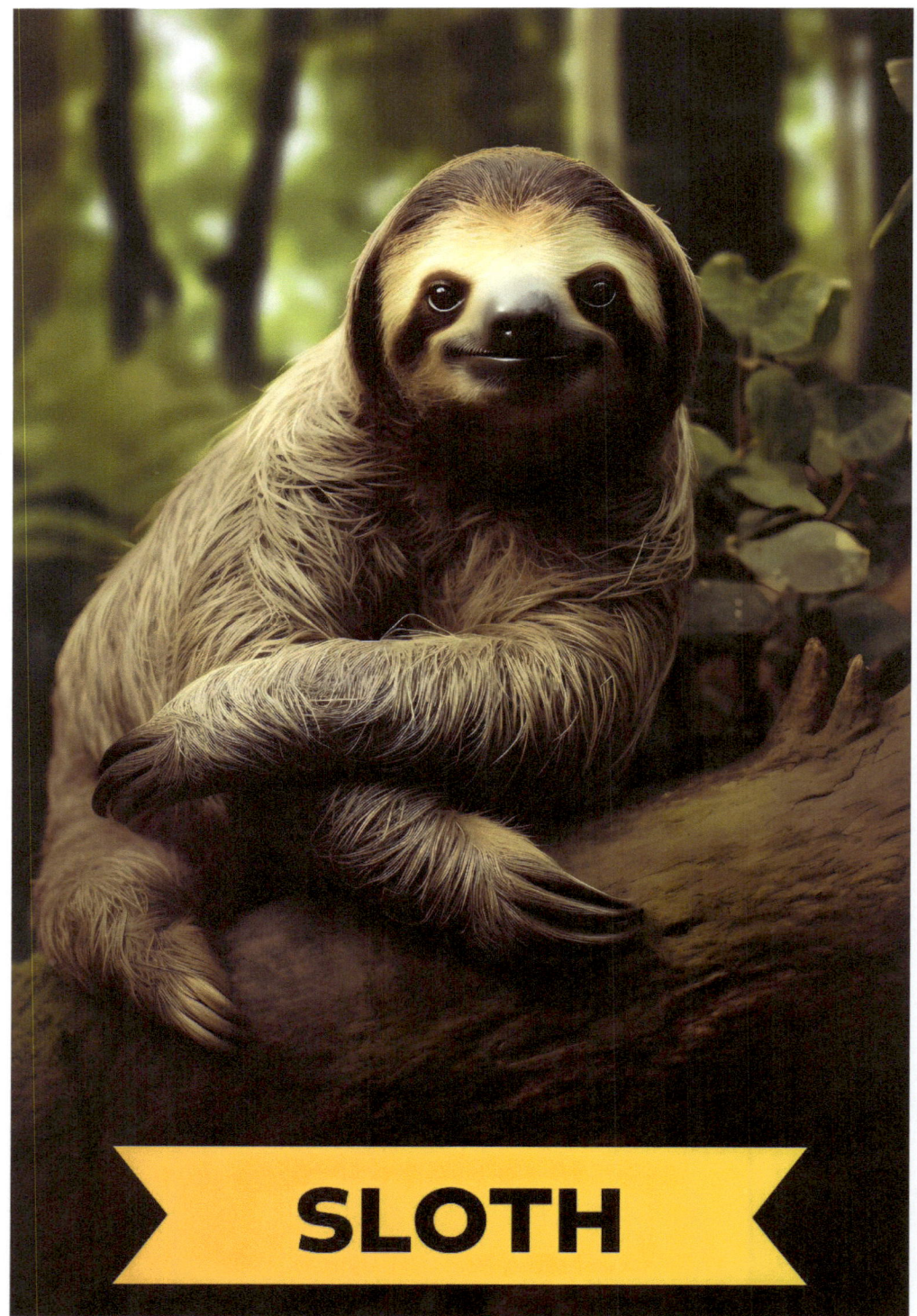

# SLOTH

# TORTOISE

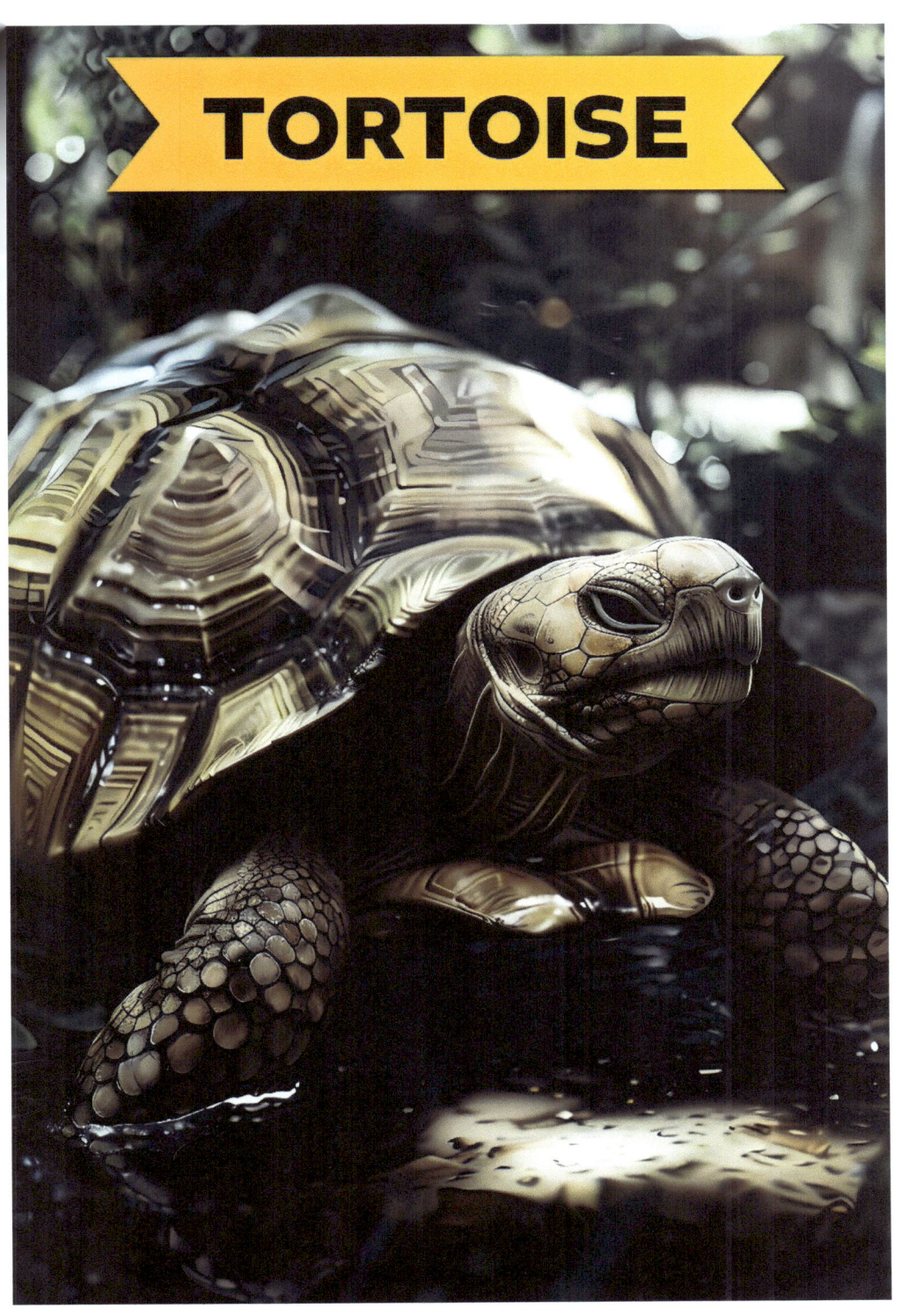

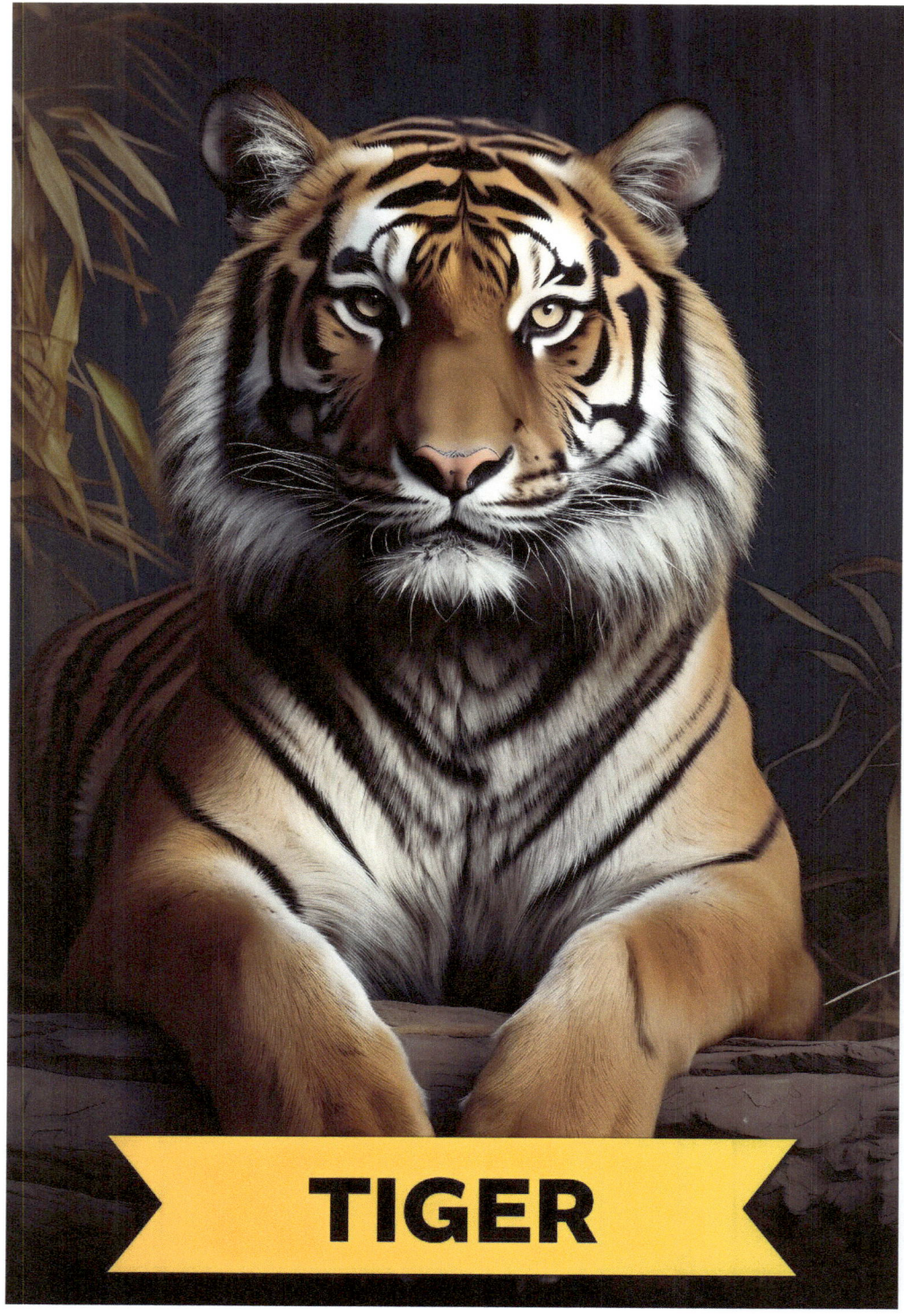

**TIGER**

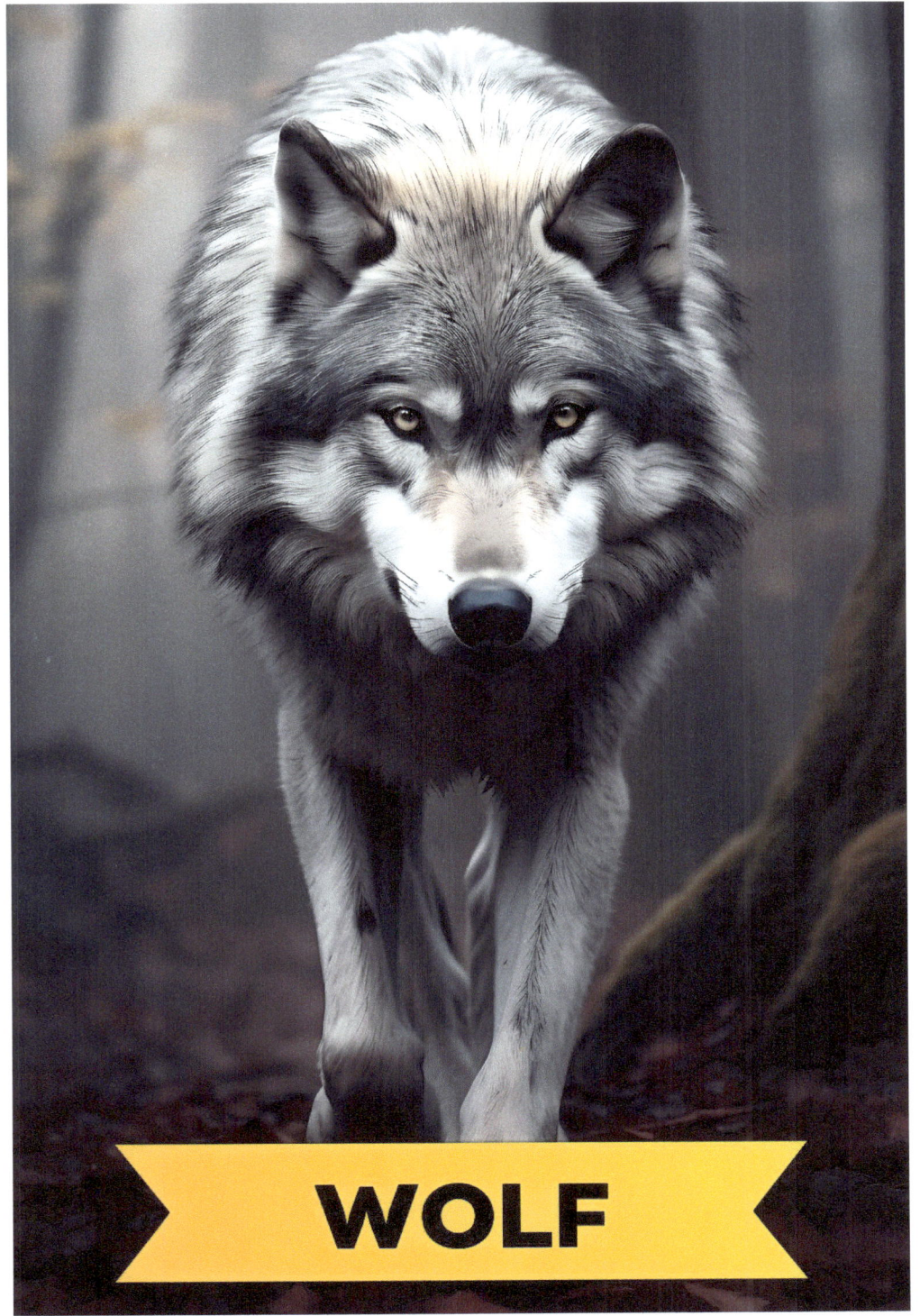

**WOLF**

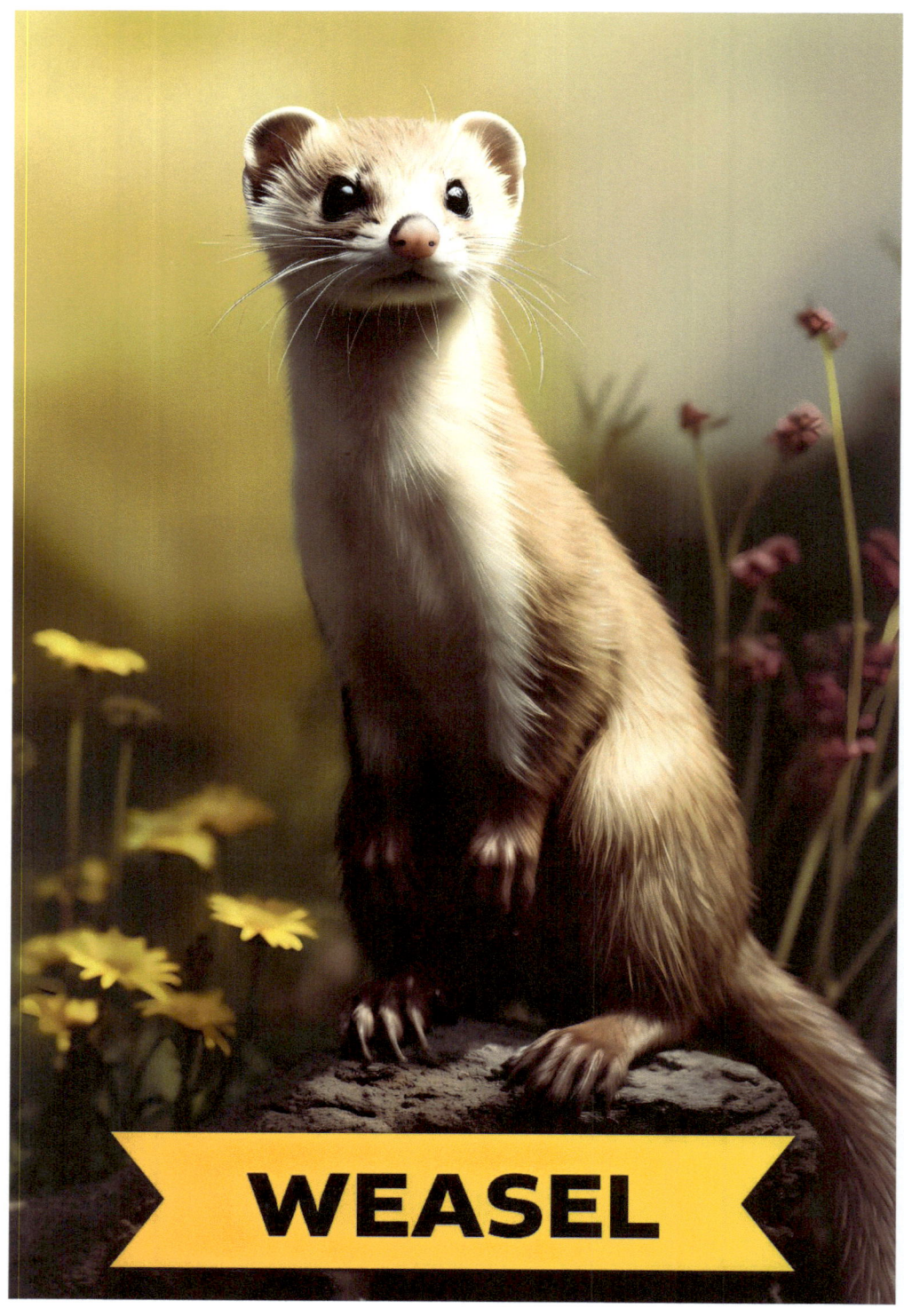

**WEASEL**

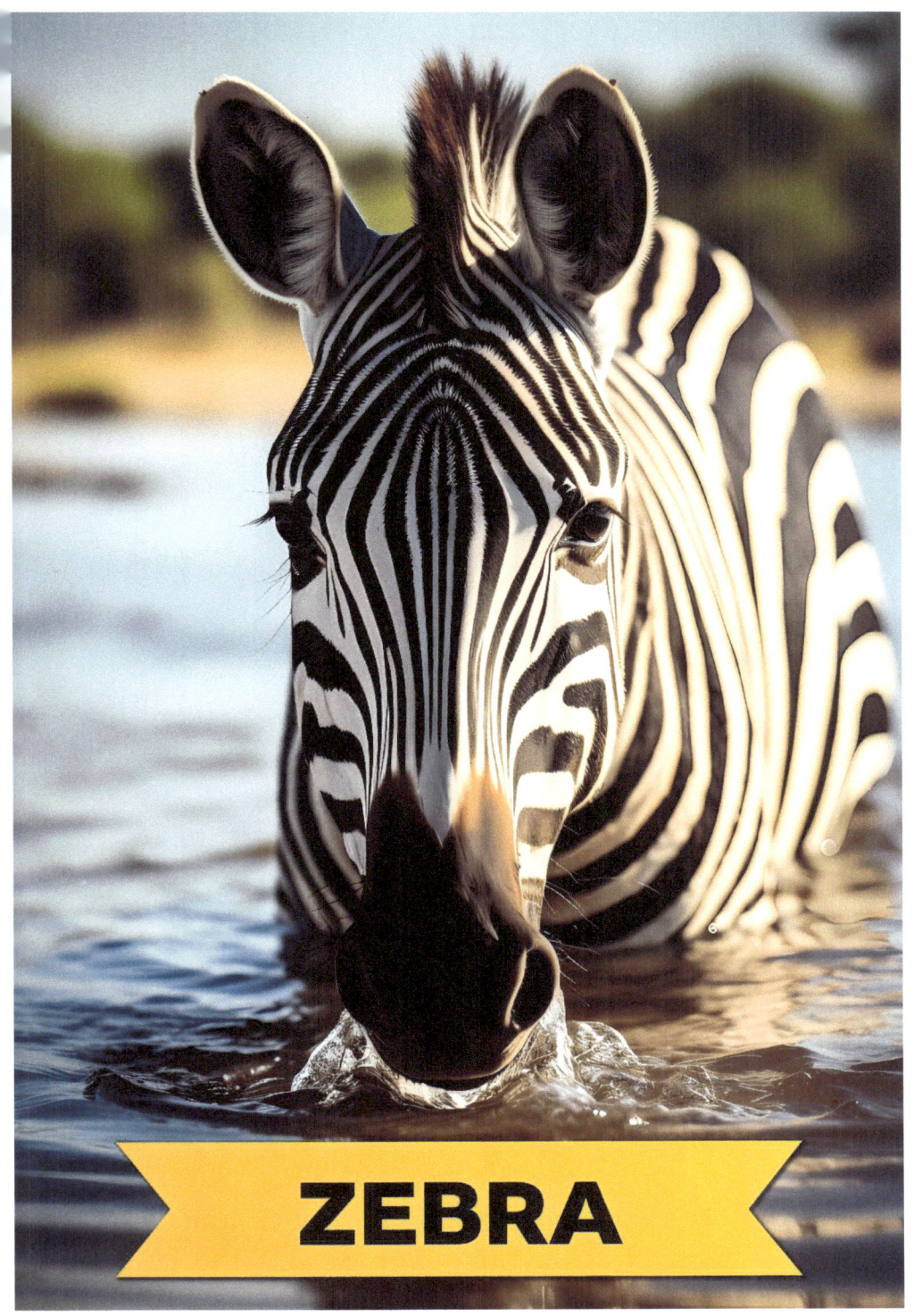

**ZEBRA**

www.ingramcontent.com/pod-product-compliance
Lightning Source LLC
Chambersburg PA
CBHW040334220526
45473CB00009B/2682